THAT'S TRUMP

MORE RECIPES FROM THE BEST OF BRIDGE

SIXTH EFFORT
"SIXTH TIME 'ROUND"

WRITTEN AND PUBLISHED BY:

THE BEST OF BRIDGE PUBLISHING LTD.
6037 - 6TH STREET S.E.
CALGARY, ALBERTA, CANADA T2H 1L8

PRINTED IN CANADA BY CENTAX BOOKS
A DIVISION OF PW GROUP

FOOD PHOTOGRAPHY BY SIMON CHEUNG

PORTRAIT PHOTOGRAPH - PHOTOS BY STEWART LTD.

NUTRITIONAL ANALYSIS BY ALVINA HILLS R.D.
SUSAN GATCHELL R.D.

SIXTH EFFORT PUBLISHED SEPTEMBER, 1995

DEDICATION

THIS BOOK IS DEDICATED TO
THE MEMORY OF
MARILYN LYLE
OUR FRIEND AND PARTNER

KAREN BRIMACOMBE   HELEN MILES

LINDA JACOBSON   VAL ROBINSON

MARY HALPEN   JOAN WILSON

CANADIAN CATALOGUING IN PUBLICATION DATA
MAIN ENTRY UNDER TITLE:
THAT'S TRUMP: MORE RECIPES FROM THE BEST OF BRIDGE

INCLUDES INDEX TO ALL OF THE PUBLISHER'S COOKBOOKS.
ISBN 0-9690425-6-6

I. LOW-FAT DIET - RECIPES   2. COOKERY
I. BEST OF BRIDGE PUBLISHING LTD.

TX714. T43 1995   641. 5'638   C95-920167-X

PEOPLE ASK, "WHAT'S IT LIKE TO WORK WITH
   THE BEST OF BRIDGE?"
THOSE AMAZING WOMEN, WHO RUN FROM THE
   STOVE TO THE FRIDGE.
WELL, I'LL GIVE YOU JUST A BIRD'S-EYE VIEW
OF WHAT THEY ARE LIKE AND WHAT THEY DO.
THEY TEST AND THEY TASTE AND ARE VERY DEMOCRATIC
THAT MEANS FIVE GIVE IN WHEN THE SIXTH IS EMPHATIC!
THEIR DECISIONS ARE BASED ON RESEARCH AND GOOD
   COMMON SENSE
NEVER TOO QUICK 'CAUSE THERE IS TIME TO SIT ON THE
   FENCE.

IS IT CARAMEL OR CARMEL, IS IT RIND OR IS IT ZEST?
SHOULD THE COVER BE PURPLE OR WOULD GREEN BE
   THE BEST?
THAT PHOTO IS GOOD BUT THIS ONE IS CONTRIVED
DO WE USE LETTUCE OR CHIVES OR MAYBE ENDIVE?
THEY'VE BEEN TO THE MARKET AT LEAST EVERY DAY
IS IT 398 mL OR JUST HOW MUCH DOES IT WEIGH?
IT'S BEEN REWRITTEN, RETESTED AND LOTS ARE
   REJECTED.
IF IT'S A FAMILY FAVORITE THEN FEELINGS ARE AFFECTED.
SET UP AND BLUELINES - STILL MORE RECIPES TO TEST
THAT ONE WON'T PASS, BUT I SERVED THIS TO MY GUESTS.
PROMOS TO THE PRESS, A PUBLIC APPEARANCE
A BUDGET TO BALANCE, WE CAN'T GIVE THAT CLEARANCE.
THE NOVICE BOOK WRITER FINDS THEM VERY APPROACHABLE
THE COMPUTER TEACHER PONDERS, THEY'RE BRIGHT BUT
   ARE THEY COACHABLE?
THERE ARE SALESMEN AND BOOKSELLERS AND THE
   HUSBAND WHO RINGS
"WHAT'S FOR DINNER? I HOPE IT'S CREAM CORN AND OTHER
   GOOD THINGS!"

WHEN THE OFFICE DOOR CLOSES THEY GO HOME AND TEST
   MORE
SO "THAT'S TRUMP" WILL BE AS GOOD AS THE BOOKS THAT
   WENT BEFORE!

   BETTY LYNN PENNINGTON
   BEST OF BRIDGE OFFICE MANAGER

THE BEST OF BRIDGE LADIES HAVE FACED THE FORMIDABLE FOE OF "FOODDOM" - FAT! ENLISTING THE SERVICES OF TWO ENTHUSIASTIC DIETITIANS, WE HAVE DEVELOPED A TASTY COLLECTION OF FAT-REDUCED RECIPES.

A HALO ⎯⊛⎯ AT THE BOTTOM OF A RECIPE

MEANS LESS THAN 15 GRAMS OF FAT PER SERVING - A HEALTHY APPROACH TO EATING. DON'T BE AFRAID TO SUBSTITUTE FAT-REDUCED INGREDIENTS IN YOUR FAVORITE RECIPES. THERE ARE MANY EXCELLENT NEW PRODUCTS AVAILABLE - JUST READ THE LABEL!

THE FOUR FOOD GROUPS: TASTY. FATTENING. YUMMY. CELERY.

PICTURED ON COVER:

CHICKEN MEDALLIONS WITH SPINACH

- PAGE 126

TABLE OF CONTENTS

SWISS BREAKFAST MUESLI

LOWER IN FAT THAN MOST GRANOLAS.

1½ CUPS ROLLED OATS, UNCOOKED	375 mL
1 CUP SKIM MILK	250 mL
1 CUP PLAIN SKIM MILK YOGURT	250 mL
3 APPLES, PEELED & GRATED	
2 TBSP. LEMON JUICE	30 mL
2 TBSP. HONEY	30 mL
½ TSP. CINNAMON	2 mL

IN A MEDIUM BOWL MIX ALL INGREDIENTS. COVER AND REFRIGERATE OVERNIGHT OR UP TO 4 DAYS. TO SERVE, SPOON MUESLI INTO CEREAL BOWLS; TOP WITH FRESH FRUIT OR RAISINS AND A DOLLOP OF LOW-FAT YOGURT. SERVES 4.

2.5 GRAMS FAT PER SERVING (INCLUDES FRUIT AND YOGURT).

BLENDER BREAKFAST

A QUICK NUTRITIOUS DRINK!

1 BANANA
6-8 STRAWBERRIES (FRESH OR FROZEN)
½ GRAPEFRUIT, PEELED
BLEND ALL FRUITS IN BLENDER UNTIL SMOOTH.

VARIATION: 1 BANANA
2 SLICES FRESH PINEAPPLE
1 ORANGE, PEELED

0 GRAMS OF FAT

PEACH AND BLUEBERRY CLAFOUTI

A DELIGHTFULLY SIMPLE BAKED PANCAKE FOR SUMMER FRUITS.

1 TBSP. BUTTER	15 mL
3 EGGS	
1/3 CUP SUGAR	75 mL
1/3 CUP HALF AND HALF CREAM	75 mL
GRATED ZEST OF 1 LEMON	
1 TSP. VANILLA	5 mL
3 TBSP. FLOUR	45 mL
2-3 PEACHES, PEELED AND SLICED	
1 CUP BLUEBERRIES	250 mL
ICING SUGAR AND LEMON JUICE	

PREHEAT OVEN TO 375°F. GENEROUSLY BUTTER A SHALLOW 10" BAKING DISH. BEAT EGGS AND SUGAR UNTIL FROTHY. ADD CREAM, LEMON ZEST AND VANILLA. MIX WELL AND ADD FLOUR. MIX UNTIL SMOOTH AND POUR BATTER INTO A BAKING DISH. SCATTER FRUIT EVENLY OVER THE BATTER. BAKE FOR ABOUT 20 MINUTES - UNTIL SET. COOL AND DUST WITH ICING SUGAR. SERVE WITH A SPRINKLE OF LEMON JUICE. SERVES 4-6.

MY GRANDMOTHER STARTED WALKING FIVE MILES A DAY WHEN SHE WAS SIXTY. SHE'S NINETY-SEVEN NOW, AND WE DON'T KNOW WHERE THE HECK SHE IS.

TOMATO, CHEESE AND HERB TART

YOU'RE RIGHT - THIS WILL TAKE SOME TIME, BUT YOUR GUESTS (AND YOUR REPUTATION) ARE WORTH IT! SERVE WITH SALAD GREENS AND BALSAMIC VINAIGRETTE (PAGE 66) AND SHRIMP AND CRAB QUICHE ("BEST OF BRIDGE" PAGE 40).

CRUST

1¼ CUPS FLOUR	300 mL
¼ TSP. SALT	1 mL
½ CUP UNSALTED BUTTER, CHILLED AND CUT INTO PIECES	125 mL
4 TBSP. ICE WATER	60 mL

FILLING

3-4 MEDIUM TOMATOES, CUT INTO ½" THICK SLICES	
9 OZ. GRUYÈRE CHEESE, THINLY SLICED	265 OZ.
1 TSP. BASIL	5 mL
1 TSP. OREGANO	5 mL
¼ TSP. THYME	1 mL
3 TBSP. FRESHLY GRATED PARMESAN CHEESE	45 mL
PEPPER	

TO MAKE CRUST: COMBINE FLOUR AND SALT IN A FOOD PROCESSOR. CUT IN BUTTER UNTIL MIXTURE RESEMBLES COARSE MEAL. ADD WATER BY TABLESPOONS UNTIL DOUGH FORMS MOIST CLUMPS. FORM INTO A BALL, WRAP IN PLASTIC AND REFRIGERATE AT LEAST 30 MINUTES. ROLL OUT DOUGH TO A 13" ROUND AND TRANSFER TO AN 11" TART PAN WITH REMOVABLE BOTTOM.

TOMATO, CHEESE AND HERB TART

THIS RECIPE CONTINUED FROM PAGE 8. FREEZE CRUST 15 MINUTES. LINE CRUST WITH FOIL AND FILL WITH DRIED BEANS OR PIE WEIGHTS. BAKE AT 375°F FOR 15 MINUTES. REMOVE BEANS AND FOIL AND BAKE ANOTHER 15 MINUTES, OR UNTIL GOLDEN. COOL ON A RACK. MAY BE PREPARED A DAY IN ADVANCE. COVER AND LET STAND AT ROOM TEMPERATURE.

TO MAKE FILLING: CUT EACH TOMATO SLICE IN HALF. PLACE SLICES ON PAPER TOWELS TO DRAIN FOR AT LEAST 45 MINUTES. PREHEAT OVEN TO 375°F. PLACE CHEESE SLICES ON CRUST. ARRANGE TOMATOES ON TOP OF CHEESE, OVERLAPPING SLIGHTLY. SPRINKLE HERBS, THEN PARMESAN OVER TOMATOES. SEASON WITH PEPPER. BAKE 30-35 MINUTES, OR UNTIL CHEESE MELTS. COOL SLIGHTLY. REMOVE TART PAN SIDES. CUT TART INTO 8 WEDGES.

MAYBE MONEY ISN'T EVERYTHING, BUT DON'T BRING THAT UP ON THE FIRST DATE.

HAVE THE SEÑOR MAKE THIS MEXICAN MARVEL - THE NEXT BRUNCH FAVORITE.

3 - 4-OZ. CANS MILD GREEN CHILIES, CHOPPED	3 - 115 g
6 CORN TORTILLAS, CUT INTO 1" STRIPS	
2 LBS. HOT ITALIAN SAUSAGE, CASING REMOVED, COOKED, DRAINED	1 kg
2½ CUPS GRATED MONTEREY JACK CHEESE	625 mL
½ CUP MILK	125 mL
8 EGGS	
½ TSP. SALT	2 mL
½ TSP. GARLIC SALT	2 mL
½ TSP. ONION SALT	2 mL
½ TSP. CUMIN	2 mL
½ TSP. FRESHLY GROUND PEPPER	2 mL
PAPRIKA TO SPRINKLE	
2 LARGE RIPE TOMATOES, SLICED	
SALSA AND SOUR CREAM FOR CONDIMENTS	

THE NIGHT BEFORE, GREASE A 9" x 13" CASSEROLE AND LAYER ½ THE CHILIES, ½ THE CORN TORTILLAS, ½ THE COOKED SAUSAGE, AND ½ THE CHEESE. REPEAT LAYERS. IN A MEDIUM BOWL, BEAT MILK, EGGS, SALT, GARLIC SALT, ONION SALT, CUMIN AND PEPPER. POUR OVER CASSEROLE INGREDIENTS. SPRINKLE WITH PAPRIKA. COVER WITH PLASTIC WRAP AND REFRIGERATE OVERNIGHT. HOORAY - IT'S THE FOLLOWING DAY, AND YOU'RE READY! PREHEAT OVEN TO 350°F. PLACE TOMATOES OVER TOP OF

WEEKEND SPOUSE SAVER

THIS RECIPE CONTINUED FROM PAGE 10.

CASSEROLE. BAKE 1 HOUR, OR UNTIL SET IN CENTER AND SLIGHTLY BROWNED AT EDGES. LET SIT 5 MINUTES BEFORE SERVING. PASS THE SALSA AND SOUR CREAM. SERVE WITH A TRAY OF SLICED FRESH FRUIT. ¡MAGNIFICO! SERVES 10.

PHYSICS LESSON; WHEN A BODY IS SUBMERGED IN WATER, THE PHONE RINGS.

SCOTTY'S NEST EGGS

ONE OF OUR FAVORITE BACHELORS LOVES TO WHIP THIS UP.

EACH NEST

2-3 THIN SLICES BLACK FOREST HAM	
1 EGG	
1 TBSP. CREAM	15 mL
1 HEAPING TBSP. GRATED SWISS CHEESE	25 mL
SPRINKLE OF BASIL	
ENGLISH MUFFIN	

PREHEAT OVEN TO 350°F. GREASE LARGE MUFFIN TINS. LINE WITH HAM AND BREAK EGG OVER TOP. ADD CREAM AND SPRINKLE WITH CHEESE AND BASIL. BAKE 12-15 MINUTES. SERVE ON HALF A TOASTED ENGLISH MUFFIN. (PLACE WATER IN ANY UNUSED MUFFIN CUPS TO PREVENT DAMAGE.) (PICTURED ON PAGE 17.)

BRIE, FRESH HERB AND TOMATO OMELETTE

4 EGGS	
2 TSP. WATER	10 mL
SALT AND PEPPER TO TASTE	
1 TBSP. BUTTER	15 mL
1 TBSP. CHOPPED FRESH CHIVES	15 mL
1 TBSP. CHOPPED FRESH DILLWEED	15 mL
1 TBSP. CHOPPED FRESH PARSLEY	15 mL
1 SMALL TOMATO, COARSELY CHOPPED	
6 SLICES (¼") BRIE CHEESE, TO COVER HALF THE OMELETTE	
1 TSP. WATER	5 mL

BEAT EGGS WITH WATER, SALT AND PEPPER UNTIL LIGHT AND FROTHY. MELT BUTTER IN A 10" HEAVY SKILLET. POUR IN EGG MIXTURE. COVER AND COOK GENTLY OVER MEDIUM HEAT UNTIL ALMOST SET. LAYER REMAINING INGREDIENTS IN ORDER OVER HALF THE OMELETTE. FOLD OVER OMELETTE. ADD WATER TO PAN, COVER AND COOK UNTIL JUST DONE (APPROXIMATELY 5 MINUTES). GENTLY SLIDE OMELETTE ONTO WARMED PLATE. MAKES 2 GENEROUS SERVINGS.

DEFINITION OF A OPTIMIST: AN ACCORDIAN PLAYER WITH A BEEPER.

THIS LAYERED SANDWICH IS KNOWN FOR ITS TANGY OLIVE SALAD FILLING. A GREAT IDEA FOR HIKERS, BIKERS, OR SANDWICH LIKERS!

10" ROUND ITALIAN LOAF

FILLING

½ CUP PIMIENTO-STUFFED GREEN OLIVES	125 mL
½ CUP PITTED BLACK OLIVES	125 mL
6½-OZ. JAR MARINATED ARTICHOKES, DRAINED	184 mL
1 GARLIC CLOVE, MINCED	
1 TBSP. MINCED JALAPEÑO PEPPER	15 mL
⅓ CUP PARSLEY, MINCED	75 mL
¼ CUP OLIVE OIL	60 mL
½ LB. GRILLED CHICKEN OR SALAMI, THINLY SLICED	250 g
½ LB. PROVOLONE, MOZZARELLA OR SWISS CHEESE, THINLY SLICED	250 g

CHOP OR PROCESS FILLING INGREDIENTS TO A SPREADABLE CONSISTENCY. CUT LOAF IN HALF HORIZONTALLY AND REMOVE ENOUGH OF THE BREAD TO LEAVE A ½" SHELL. SPREAD BOTTOM SHELL WITH HALF THE FILLING, LAYER MEAT AND CHEESE SLICES THEN TOP WITH REMAINING FILLING. PRESS TOP OF LOAF ON SANDWICH AND WRAP TIGHTLY IN PLASTIC WRAP. PLACE SOMETHING HEAVY (LIKE A DICTIONARY) ON TOP TO COMPRESS SANDWICH AND CHILL FOR SEVERAL HOURS. CUT IN WEDGES WITH A SERRATED KNIFE. SERVES 8-10. (PICTURED ON PAGE 71.)

CRANAPPLE COFFEECAKE

MOIST AND PERFECT FOR BRUNCH.

2 CUPS FLOUR	500 mL
1½ TSP. BAKING SODA	7 mL
1 TSP. CINNAMON	5 mL
½ TSP. BAKING POWDER	2 mL
½ TSP. SALT	2 mL
1¼ CUPS UNSWEETENED APPLESAUCE	300 mL
1 CUP PACKED BROWN SUGAR	250 mL
2 LARGE EGG WHITES	
½ CUP OIL	125 mL
1 CUP HALVED FRESH OR FROZEN CRANBERRIES	250 mL
1 CUP COARSELY GRATED RED APPLE	250 mL

ICING

JUICE & GRATED RIND OF 1 ORANGE	
1 CUP ICING SUGAR	250 mL

PREHEAT OVEN TO 325°F. GREASE AND FLOUR A BUNDT PAN. COMBINE FLOUR, BAKING SODA, CINNAMON, BAKING POWDER AND SALT. IN A LARGE BOWL, BEAT APPLESAUCE, BROWN SUGAR, EGG WHITES AND OIL THOROUGHLY. BEAT IN FLOUR MIXTURE UNTIL SMOOTH. FOLD IN CRANBERRIES AND APPLE. POUR BATTER IN BUNDT PAN; BAKE 45-55 MINUTES, OR UNTIL CAKE TESTER COMES OUT CLEAN. COOL IN PAN ON A RACK FOR 10 MINUTES. INVERT PAN AND PLACE CAKE ON RACK TO COOL.

TO MAKE ICING: BRING JUICE AND RIND TO A BOIL AND SIMMER FOR 1 MINUTE. BEAT IN ICING SUGAR UNTIL SMOOTH. DRIZZLE OVER CAKE. CUT INTO 16 SLICES.

7 GRAMS FAT PER SLICE

¾ CUP BUTTERMILK OR PLAIN YOGURT	175 mL
1 EGG	
2¾ CUPS FLOUR	675 mL
4 TSP. BAKING POWDER	20 mL
½ TSP. BAKING SODA	2 mL
½ TSP. SALT	2 mL
½ CUP MARGARINE	125 mL
1 CUP COARSELY CHOPPED CRANBERRIES	250 mL
(FRESH OR FROZEN)	
½ CUP SUGAR	125 mL
RIND OF 1 ORANGE	
1 TBSP. BUTTER, MELTED	15 mL
¼ CUP ICING SUGAR	60 mL

PREHEAT OVEN TO 375°F. BEAT BUTTERMILK AND EGG IN SMALL BOWL AND SET ASIDE. IN LARGE BOWL, MEASURE FLOUR, BAKING POWDER, BAKING SODA AND SALT. CUT IN MARGARINE UNTIL MIXTURE RESEMBLES SMALL PEAS. MIX IN CRANBERRIES, SUGAR AND ORANGE RIND. ADD BUTTERMILK MIXTURE AND STIR UNTIL SOFT DOUGH FORMS. USING YOUR HANDS, FORM DOUGH INTO A LARGE BALL AND PLACE ON FLOURED SURFACE. PAT OUT TO 1" THICKNESS. CUT IN 4" ROUNDS. PLACE ON UNGREASED COOKIE SHEET AND BAKE SCONES FOR 15-20 MINUTES. WHILE STILL WARM, BRUSH WITH BUTTER AND SPRINKLE WITH ICING SUGAR. MAKES 8 LARGE SCONES.

GENTLEMEN PREFER BONDS.

STRAWBERRY MUFFINS

2 CUPS FLOUR	500 mL
½ CUP SUGAR	125 mL
⅓ CUP DRY SKIM MILK POWDER	75 mL
1 TBSP. BAKING POWDER	15 mL
½ TSP. SALT	2 mL
1 EGG	
½ CUP MARGARINE, MELTED	125 mL
½ CUP SKIM MILK	125 mL
1 CUP CHOPPED FRESH STRAWBERRIES	250 mL
1 TSP. LEMON JUICE	5 mL
½ TSP. GRATED LEMON RIND	2 mL

PREHEAT OVEN TO 400°F. IN LARGE BOWL, COMBINE FLOUR, SUGAR, SKIM MILK POWDER, BAKING POWDER AND SALT. IN A MEDIUM BOWL, BEAT EGG, MARGARINE AND MILK UNTIL WELL BLENDED. ADD STRAWBERRIES, LEMON JUICE AND RIND. POUR LIQUID MIXTURE INTO DRY INGREDIENTS AND STIR GENTLY JUST UNTIL DRY INGREDIENTS ARE MOISTENED. SPOON BATTER EVENLY INTO 12 LIGHTLY SPRAYED MUFFIN CUPS. BAKE FOR 15-20 MINUTES, OR UNTIL TOOTHPICK COMES OUT CLEAN AND THEY ARE GOLDEN BROWN. MAKES 12 MUFFINS.

MY WIFE THINKS I'M NOSEY. AT LEAST THAT'S WHAT SHE SAYS IN HER DIARY.

PICTURED ON OVERLEAF

SCOTTY'S NEST EGGS - PAGE 11
ROASTED ORANGE PEPPER AND CORN
SALSA - PAGE 93

RASPBERRY-FILLED CINNAMON MUFFINS

A LOW-FAT JAM SESSION

MUFFINS

1½ CUPS FLOUR	375 mL
½ CUP SUGAR	125 mL
2½ TSP. BAKING POWDER	12 mL
1 TSP. CINNAMON	5 mL
¼ TSP. SALT	1 mL
⅔ CUP BUTTERMILK	150 mL
¼ CUP MARGARINE, MELTED	60 mL
1 EGG, SLIGHTLY BEATEN	
¼ CUP RASPBERRY JAM	60 mL

TOPPING

1 TBSP. SUGAR	15 mL
¼ TSP. CINNAMON	1 mL

PREHEAT OVEN TO 400°F. COMBINE FLOUR, SUGAR, BAKING POWDER, CINNAMON AND SALT. MAKE A WELL IN CENTER OF MIXTURE. MIX BUTTERMILK, MARGARINE AND EGG AND STIR WELL. ADD TO THE FLOUR MIXTURE, STIRRING JUST UNTIL MOISTENED. SPRAY 12 MUFFIN TINS WITH VEGETABLE COOKING SPRAY AND SPOON ABOUT 1 TBSP. BATTER INTO EACH ONE. SPOON 1 TSP. JAM INTO CENTER OF EACH MUFFIN CUP (DON'T SPREAD OVER BATTER) AND TOP WITH REMAINING BATTER. COMBINE TOPPING MIXTURE AND SPRINKLE EVENLY OVER MUFFINS. BAKE FOR 20 MINUTES, OR UNTIL MUFFINS SPRING BACK WHEN TOUCHED LIGHTLY IN CENTER. REMOVE MUFFINS FROM PAN IMMEDIATELY, AND COOL ON WIRE RACK. MAKES 12 MUFFINS.

4.5 GRAMS FAT PER MUFFIN

YOU'LL LUV THESE!

1½ CUPS FLOUR	375 mL
1 TSP. BAKING POWDER	5 mL
1 TSP. BAKING SODA	5 mL
½ TSP. SALT	2 mL
½ TSP. CINNAMON	2 mL
¼ TSP. NUTMEG	1 mL
⅛ TSP. GINGER	0.5 mL
⅛ TSP. ALLSPICE	0.5 mL
¾ CUP BROWN SUGAR	175 mL
1 EGG	
½ CUP 1% BUTTERMILK	125 mL
OR PLAIN SKIM MILK YOGURT	
¼ CUP OIL	60 mL
½ TSP. VANILLA	2 mL
14-OZ. CAN CRUSHED PINEAPPLE,	398 mL
DRAINED	
¾ CUP FINELY GRATED CARROTS	175 mL
½ CUP RAISINS	125 mL

PREHEAT OVEN TO 400°F. LIGHTLY SPRAY 12 MUFFIN CUPS OR LINE WITH PAPER CUPS. USING A FORK, STIR FLOUR WITH BAKING POWDER, BAKING SODA, SALT, SPICES AND SUGAR IN A LARGE MIXING BOWL. WHISK EGG IN A MEDIUM-SIZE BOWL WITH BUTTERMILK, OIL AND VANILLA. STIR IN PINEAPPLE. POUR INTO FLOUR MIXTURE AND STIR JUST UNTIL COMBINED. STIR IN CARROTS AND RAISINS. SPOON BATTER INTO MUFFIN CUPS. BAKE 15-17 MINUTES OR UNTIL A TOOTHPICK COMES OUT CLEAN. THESE MAY BE FROZEN - IF YOUR FAMILY DOESN'T FIND THEM FIRST! MAKES 12 MUFFINS.

5.4 GRAMS FAT PER MUFFIN

THESE TASTE GREAT EVEN WHEN THEY'RE SQUASHED! A MAKE-AHEAD MIX FOR 3 DOZEN MUFFINS.

3 CUPS FLOUR	750 mL
3 CUPS ROLLED OATS	750 mL
4 TSP. BAKING POWDER	20 mL
1½ TSP. SALT	7 mL
1 TSP. NUTMEG	5 mL
1 TSP. CINNAMON	5 mL
¾ CUP BROWN SUGAR	175 mL
¾ CUP WHITE SUGAR	175 mL
1½ CUPS MARGARINE	375 mL
1 CUP FLAKED ALMONDS	250 mL
1½ CUPS CHOPPED DATES	375 mL
1½ CUPS CHOPPED DRIED APRICOTS	375 mL
RIND OF 1 ORANGE	

FOR ONE BATCH:

1¼ CUPS BUTTERMILK	300 mL
1 EGG, BEATEN	

USING AN EXTRA-LARGE BOWL OR ROASTING PAN, MIX FLOUR, OATS, BAKING POWDER, SALT, NUTMEG, CINNAMON AND SUGARS TOGETHER. CUT IN MARGARINE USING PASTRY BLENDER. ADD ALMONDS, DATES, APRICOTS AND ORANGE RIND. MEASURE INTO 3 EQUAL BATCHES (APPROXIMATELY 4 CUPS EACH) AND STORE IN REFRIGERATOR UP TO 4 WEEKS.

WHEN READY TO MAKE MUFFINS, ADD BUTTERMILK AND EGG TO 1 BATCH OF MUFFIN MIXTURE. MIX AND SPOON INTO PAPER-LINED MUFFIN TINS. BAKE AT 350°F FOR 20 MINUTES. MAKES 12 MEDIUM MUFFINS.

GUILT-REDUCED BRAN MUFFINS

TASTY LITTLE DEVILS - YOU'LL LOVE THE MARMALADE.

1/4 CUP MARGARINE	60 mL
1/2 CUP PACKED BROWN SUGAR	125 mL
6 TBSP. MOLASSES	90 mL
1/4 CUP MARMALADE	60 mL
2 EGGS, BEATEN	
1 CUP SKIM MILK	250 mL
1 1/2 CUPS NATURAL BRAN	375 mL
1 CUP WHOLE WHEAT FLOUR	250 mL
1 1/2 TSP. BAKING POWDER	7 mL
2/3 CUP RAISINS OR CHOPPED DATES OR CHOPPED DRIED APRICOTS	150 mL

PREHEAT OVEN TO 350°F. CREAM MARGARINE AND BROWN SUGAR. ADD MOLASSES, MARMALADE AND EGGS, BEAT TO COMBINE, ADD MILK AND MIX AGAIN. ADD BRAN, FLOUR AND BAKING POWDER. STIR TO COMBINE AND FOLD IN RAISINS. SPOON BATTER INTO LIGHTLY SPRAYED MUFFIN CUPS. BAKE FOR 15 MINUTES. MAKES 12 LARGE MUFFINS.

5.2 GRAMS FAT PER MUFFIN

TOURIST WRITING TO FRIEND: "ONCE AGAIN, OUR VACATION HAS ENDED THE DROUGHT OF THE CENTURY!"

SUE'S BAGUETTE X TWO

SHE'S A CRAFTY LADY!
FRESH BREAD IN LESS THAN 2 HOURS!

2 TBSP. SUGAR	30 mL
1 TBSP. SALT	15 mL
1 TBSP. YEAST	15 mL
2½ CUPS WARM WATER	625 mL
6 CUPS WHITE FLOUR	1.5 L
1 EGG WHITE	

MIX SUGAR, SALT AND YEAST TOGETHER. ADD
WATER AND LET SIT 5 MINUTES. WORK IN FLOUR 1
CUP AT A TIME AND KNEAD WELL. LET RISE
UNTIL DOUBLE. PUNCH DOWN AND FORM INTO
2 LONG LOAVES. PLACE ON A WELL-GREASED
BAKING SHEET. SLASH, BRUSH WITH EGG WHITE.
COVER LIGHTLY WITH A TEA TOWEL. LET DOUGH
RISE AGAIN. BAKE AT 425°F FOR 10 MINUTES,
THEN LOWER HEAT TO 350°F FOR 25 MINUTES.

☀ JUST A TRACE OF FAT!

YOU KNOW YOU'VE SPENT TOO MUCH MONEY ON YOUR
VACATION WHEN THE BALANCE IN YOUR BANK ACCOUNT
IS LOWER THAN THE NUMBER ON YOUR SUNSCREEN.

OLIVE, ONION AND ROSEMARY FOCACCIA

HOW DID THAT LITTLE ONION GET IN THERE WITH THOSE TWO LONELY LITTLE PETUNIAS?

2½ TSP. YEAST	12 mL
1¾ CUPS WARM WATER	425 mL
1 TSP. SUGAR	5 mL
4½-5 CUPS FLOUR	1.125-1.25 L
1¼ TSP. SALT	6 mL
3 TBSP. OLIVE OIL, DIVIDED	45 mL
2 TSP. FINELY CHOPPED FRESH ROSEMARY	10 mL
½ LB. KALAMATA (GREEK) OLIVES, PITTED AND CUT INTO SLIVERS	250 g
¼ CUP MINCED ONION	60 mL
1½ TSP. COARSE SALT OR TO TASTE	7 mL
ROSEMARY TO SPRINKLE	

ADD YEAST AND SUGAR TO WARM WATER AND LET STAND FOR 5 MINUTES. WORK IN 4½ CUPS OF FLOUR, SALT AND 2 TBSP. OF THE OIL. KNEAD DOUGH, ADDING AS MUCH OF REMAINING ½ CUP FLOUR AS NECESSARY TO FORM SOFT DOUGH. TRANSFER TO A LIGHTLY OILED BOWL AND TURN TO COAT WITH OIL. COVER AND LET RISE IN A WARM PLACE FOR 1 HOUR, OR UNTIL DOUBLED IN SIZE. KNEAD IN THE ROSEMARY AND SOME OF THE SLIVERED OLIVES. WITH LIGHTLY OILED HANDS PRESS THE DOUGH INTO A WELL-OILED 10" X 15" JELLY ROLL PAN AND LET RISE FOR 30 MINUTES. DIMPLE THE DOUGH WITH YOUR FINGERS MAKING ¼" DEEP INDENTATIONS. BRUSH WITH REMAINING OIL AND TOP WITH ONION, REMAINING OLIVES, SALT AND ROSEMARY. BAKE AT 400°F. FOR APPROXIMATELY 30-40 MINUTES. (PICTURED ON PAGE 123.)

TEXAS TOAST

A GREAT SIDE ORDER FOR YOUR NEXT BARBECUE.

½ CUP BUTTER SOFTENED	125 mL
1-2 GARLIC CLOVES, CRUSHED	
2-3 TSP. HOT PEPPER SAUCE	10-15 mL
BAGUETTE SLICES	

MIX BUTTER, GARLIC AND PEPPER SAUCE. SPREAD ON BAGUETTE SLICES AND BROIL UNTIL GOLDEN.

IF IT ISN'T ONE THING, IT'S YOUR MOTHER!

MELBA HERB TOAST

SOUNDS LIKE WE JUST NAMED A PERSON! SERVE WITH SOUP.

½ CUP BUTTER, SOFTENED	125 mL
2 TSP. PARSLEY	10 mL
1 TSP. BASIL	5 mL
¾ TSP. OREGANO	3 mL
¾ TSP. TARRAGON	3 mL
½ TSP. GARLIC SALT	2 mL
7-OZ. PKG. MELBA TOAST SLICES	200 g

PREHEAT OVEN TO 350°F. COMBINE BUTTER WITH HERBS AND GARLIC SALT. SPREAD THINLY ON MELBA TOAST. PLACE ON A COOKIE SHEET AND BAKE FOR ABOUT 8 MINUTES.

SAVORY CHEDDAR BISCUITS

½ CUP BUTTER, SOFTENED	125 mL
2½ CUPS GRATED	625 mL
OLD CHEDDAR CHEESE	
2 TBSP. DIJON MUSTARD	30 mL
1¼ CUPS FLOUR	300 mL
½ TSP. SALT	2 mL
¼ TSP. CAYENNE PEPPER	1 mL
2 TBSP. SESAME SEEDS (OPTIONAL)	30 mL
3 TBSP. DIJON MUSTARD (OPTIONAL)	45 mL

CREAM BUTTER UNTIL SOFT AND FLUFFY. ADD CHEESE AND MUSTARD AND MIX WELL. COMBINE FLOUR, SALT AND CAYENNE AND ADD TO CHEESE MIXTURE. COMBINE UNTIL DOUGH JUST HOLDS TOGETHER. DIVIDE DOUGH INTO 2. ROLL INTO 2 LOGS ABOUT 1" IN DIAMETER. IF USING MUSTARD AND SESAME SEEDS ROLL TO COAT AT THIS TIME. FREEZE FOR 30 MINUTES TO MAKE CUTTING EASIER. CUT SLICES ¼" THICK AND PLACE ON UNGREASED BAKING SHEETS ABOUT 2" APART. BAKE AT 375°F FOR 12-15 MINUTES, OR UNTIL LIGHTLY GOLDEN. COOL ON RACK. MAKES ABOUT 48 BISCUITS.

AFTER 15 YEARS AS A DEDICATED EMPLOYEE, I WAS CANNED, DISMISSED, LET GO, DISCHARGED, AND FIRED FROM MY JOB AT THE THESAURUS COMPANY.

PEACH FROSTY

2 - 10-OZ. PKGS. FROZEN PEACH SLICES (PARTIALLY THAWED)	2 - 283 g
6-OZ. CAN FROZEN LEMONADE CONCENTRATE (PARTIALLY THAWED)	178 mL
2/3 CUP RUM	150 mL
12 ICE CUBES	

IN BLENDER, COMBINE ALL INGREDIENTS EXCEPT ICE CUBES. COVER AND BLEND ON MEDIUM-LOW SPEED FOR 30 SECONDS. ADD ICE CUBES 1 AT A TIME, BLENDING ON LOW UNTIL SLUSHY. POUR INTO NONMETAL CONTAINER.

STORE IN FREEZER. SERVES 6 - HOPEFULLY!

MONEY WON'T BUY FRIENDSHIP, BUT A GOOD SET OF JUMPER CABLES WILL.

FALLEN ANGELS

TO BE A "FALLEN ANGEL" YOU HAVE TO OWN A CAPPUCCINO MAKER.

1/4 CUP FRANGELICO	60 mL
1/4 CUP VODKA	60 mL
1/4 CUP MILK - STEAMED	60 mL

MIX EQUAL PORTIONS OF VODKA AND FRANGELICO. ADD STEAMED MILK. ADD MORE MILK IF YOU DON'T WANT TO GO TO THE DEVIL! THIS IS ONE DRINK - THE REST IS UP TO YOU!

HOT STUFF! PURISTS SAY YOU MUST SERVE WITH CELERY STICKS AND BLUE CHEESE DRESSING - SO DO IT!

CELERY STICKS, CUT IN STRIPS, STORE IN ICE WATER IN REFRIGERATOR

BLUE CHEESE DRESSING

1 OZ. BLUE CHEESE, CRUMBLED	30 g
¼ CUP MAYONNAISE (NOT MIRACLE WHIP)	60 mL
¼ CUP SOUR CREAM OR YOGURT	60 mL
¼ CUP BUTTER	60 mL
3-5 TBSP. HOT RED PEPPER SAUCE	45-75 mL
1½ TBSP. RED WINE VINEGAR	22 mL
OIL FOR DEEP-FRYING	
2½ LBS. CHICKEN WINGS, TIPS REMOVED AND CUT IN 2	1.25 kg

PREPARE CELERY STICKS. MIX DRESSING INGREDIENTS IN FOOD PROCESSOR AND CHILL UNTIL SERVING TIME. MELT BUTTER IN LARGE SAUCEPAN. STIR IN HOT SAUCE (3 TBSP. IS RELATIVELY MILD) AND VINEGAR. SET ASIDE. HEAT OIL IN A LARGE HEAVY FRYING PAN OR WOK (HOT ENOUGH WHEN A PIECE OF POTATO CRISPS QUICKLY). ADD WINGS A FEW AT A TIME, COOKING ABOUT 10 MINUTES, OR UNTIL BROWN AND CRISP. REMOVE TO A PAPER TOWEL TO DRAIN. WHEN ALL WINGS ARE COOKED, REHEAT HOT SAUCE AND TOSS WITH WINGS TO COAT.

EL GRANDO CHICKEN QUESADILLAS

Not your ordinary quesadilla, it's a knife and forker!

1 mild green chili	
1/2 red pepper	
1/2 yellow pepper	
1 whole chicken breast, boned and skinned	
1/2 tsp. chili powder	2 mL
1/2 tsp. cumin	2 mL
salt and freshly ground pepper to taste	
2 - 10" flour tortillas	2 - 25 cm
1/3 cup grated Monterey Jack cheese	75 mL
1/3 cup grated Jalapeño Jack cheese	75 mL
1/4 cup diced ripe papaya	60 mL

FOR GARNISH

1/4 cup guacamole	60 mL
1/4 cup sour cream	60 mL
1/4 cup chunky salsa	60 mL

Roast the chili and peppers under the broiler until charred. Put in a plastic bag and let stand 10 minutes to steam. Cool, peel and dice. Season chicken with chili powder, cumin, salt and pepper. Grill chicken until just opaque throughout. Cut into thin strips. Place tortilla on medium hot grill or in skillet over medium-high heat. Sprinkle with half of the cheeses, diced chili peppers, papayas and warm chicken. When cheese is melted and tortilla is lightly browned, fold tortilla in half and place in oven to keep warm. Repeat with second tortilla. Cut each quesadilla into 4 wedges. Garnish with guacamole, sour cream and salsa. Serve immediately. (Pictured on page 35.)

CURRIED CHICKEN TRIANGLES

WRAP YOUR TASTE BUDS AROUND THIS ONE.

2 TSP. MARGARINE	10 mL
½ MEDIUM ONION, FINELY CHOPPED	
½ CUP FINELY CHOPPED CELERY	125 mL
1 TBSP. FLOUR	15 mL
1½ TSP. CURRY POWDER	7 mL
¼ TSP. SALT	1 mL
½ CUP CHICKEN STOCK	125 mL
1½ CUPS DICED COOKED CHICKEN	375 mL
¼ CUP 7% SOUR CREAM	60 mL
¼ CUP SKIM MILK YOGURT	60 mL
PHYLLO PASTRY, THAWED (ABOUT ⅓ OF PACKAGE)	
¼ CUP MELTED BUTTER	60 mL

MELT MARGARINE IN SAUCEPAN. ADD ONION AND CELERY AND COOK UNTIL SOFT. ADD FLOUR, CURRY POWDER AND SALT. STIR FOR 1 MINUTE. ADD CHICKEN STOCK AND SIMMER FOR 2 MINUTES. REMOVE FROM HEAT AND ADD CHICKEN, SOUR CREAM AND YOGURT. TO MAKE TRIANGLES, UNROLL PHYLLO AND LAY FLAT. CUT A 2" WIDE STRIP. COVER THE REST OF THE PHYLLO WITH A DAMP CLOTH. BRUSH THE SINGLE STRIP WITH BUTTER. PLACE 1 TSP. OF FILLING IN BOTTOM CORNER OF STRIP AND FOLD CORNER TO CORNER (FLAG FASHION) USING ENTIRE STRIP. FILLING SHOULD BE COMPLETELY SEALED IN. CONTINUE UNTIL ALL FILLING IS USED. BRUSH TRIANGLES WITH BUTTER AND BAKE IN 350°F OVEN FOR 20-25 MINUTES. MAKES ABOUT 50.

TO FREEZE: BEFORE BAKING, FREEZE ON BAKING SHEET AND PLACE FROZEN TRIANGLES IN PLASTIC BAGS. NO NEED TO THAW BEFORE COOKING.

1.5 GRAMS FAT PER TRIANGLE

TOUCHDOWN!

1 ROUND SOURDOUGH LOAF	
2 CUPS GRATED SHARP CHEDDAR CHEESE	500 mL
1½ CUPS SOUR CREAM	375 mL
8 OZ. CREAM CHEESE	250 g
1 BUNCH GREEN ONIONS, CHOPPED	
1 TBSP. WORCESTERSHIRE SAUCE	15 mL
1 CUP SHREDDED CORNED BEEF	250 mL
4-OZ. CAN DICED GREEN CHILIES	114 mL
2-OZ. JAR PIMIENTOS, DRAINED AND CHOPPED	60 mL

CAREFULLY SLICE TOP OFF BREAD LOAF. USING A SHARP KNIFE, SLICE AROUND RIM LEAVING ½" SIDES. PULL OUT BREAD AND CUT INTO 1" CUBES. TOAST BREAD CUBES ON A COOKIE SHEET FOR 15 MINUTES AT 350°F. SET ASIDE. COMBINE REMAINING INGREDIENTS. FILL HOLLOWED LOAF WITH CHEESE MIXTURE. PLACE TOP SLICE ON LOAF AND WRAP IN FOIL. BAKE 1½ TO 2 HOURS AT 325°F. SERVE WARM WITH TOASTED BREAD CUBES AND TORTILLA CHIPS FOR DIPPING. BREAK UP THE CRUST AND EAT IT TOO.

HUSBAND TO WIFE WITH HEAD FULL OF CURLERS "WHAT ARE YOU DOING TO YOUR HAIR?"

WIFE: "I'M SETTING IT."

HUSBAND: "WHAT TIME DOES IT GO OFF?"

CHRISTINE'S CROSTINI

A HEARTY APPETIZER WITH GREAT ITALIAN FLAVOR!

½ LB. SPICY ITALIAN SAUSAGE	250 g
½ CUP CHOPPED ONION	125 mL
2 GARLIC CLOVES, MINCED	
1 MEDIUM TOMATO, CHOPPED	
1 TBSP. CHOPPED FRESH BASIL	15 mL
1 TSP. FENNEL SEEDS	5 mL
½ CUP RICOTTA CHEESE	125 mL
¼ CUP FRESHLY GRATED PARMESAN CHEESE	60 mL
1 BAGUETTE, SLICED	

REMOVE SAUSAGE MEAT FROM CASINGS AND BROWN. DRAIN MEAT AND PLACE IN MIXING BOWL. USING THE SAME FRYING PAN, SAUTÉ ONION AND GARLIC UNTIL SOFT; ADD TO SAUSAGE. ADD REMAINING INGREDIENTS TO SAUSAGE MIXTURE AND MIX WELL. (THIS CAN BE STORED IN THE REFRIGERATOR.) WHEN READY TO SERVE, SPREAD ON BAGUETTE SLICES AND PLACE UNDER BROILER UNTIL BUBBLY AND SLIGHTLY BROWNED.

NOTHING MAKES IT EASIER TO RESIST TEMPTATION THAN A PROPER UPBRINGING, A SOUND SET OF VALUES AND WITNESSES.

½ RED PEPPER	
2 TSP. FLOUR	10 mL
¼ TSP. THYME	1 mL
¼ TSP. PEPPER	1 mL
1 EGG, BEATEN	
14-OZ. CAN ARTICHOKES, DRAINED, CHOPPED	398 mL
7-OZ. CAN CRAB MEAT, DRAINED	200 g
2 TSP. LEMON JUICE	10 mL
32 WONTON WRAPPERS (3¼" X 3")	
3 TBSP. GRATED PARMESAN CHEESE	45 mL
2 TBSP. CHOPPED CHIVES	30 mL
1 TBSP. MARGARINE, MELTED	15 mL

ROAST PEPPER UNDER BROILER UNTIL CHARRED. PUT IN A PLASTIC BAG AND LET STAND FOR 10 MINUTES TO STEAM. COOL, PEEL AND CHOP. COMBINE FLOUR, THYME, PEPPER AND EGG IN A BOWL AND STIR WELL. ADD CHOPPED PEPPER, ARTICHOKES, CRAB AND LEMON JUICE. MIX THOROUGHLY. COAT 32 MINIATURE MUFFIN CUPS WITH COOKING SPRAY. GENTLY PRESS 1 WONTON WRAPPER INTO EACH CUP, ALLOWING ENDS TO EXTEND ABOVE EDGES OF CUPS. SPOON MIXTURE EVENLY INTO WRAPPERS. SPRINKLE WITH CHEESE AND CHIVES. BRUSH EDGES OF WRAPPERS WITH MELTED MARGARINE. BAKE AT 350°F FOR 15-20 MINUTES, OR UNTIL MIXTURE IS SET AND EDGES OF WRAPPERS ARE LIGHTLY BROWNED. CAN BE PREPARED EARLY IN THE DAY, REFRIGERATED AND BAKED JUST BEFORE SERVING. FREEZING IS NOT RECOMMENDED. MAKES 32 TASTY BITES.

LESS THAN 1 GRAM FAT PER "TART"

BRIE AND PAPAYA QUESADILLAS

BET YOU HAVEN'T THOUGHT OF THIS ONE - A GREAT COMBINATION!

½ CUP BOILING WATER	125 mL
1 SMALL YELLOW ONION, THINLY SLICED AND HALVED	
5 FLOUR TORTILLAS	
⅓ LB. BRIE, CUT IN ¼" STRIPS	140 g
2 JALAPEÑO PEPPERS, DICED	
1 RIPE PAPAYA, PEELED, SEEDED AND DICED	
2 TBSP. BUTTER, MELTED WITH	30 mL
2 TBSP. OIL	30 mL

POUR BOILING WATER OVER ONIONS, COVER AND LET SIT UNTIL WILTED (ABOUT 10 MINUTES). DRAIN AND SET ASIDE. ON HALF OF EACH TORTILLA PLACE A FEW STRIPS OF CHEESE, SEVERAL ONION STRIPS, A SPRINKLING OF PEPPERS AND PAPAYA. FOLD OVER AND BRUSH WITH BUTTER-OIL MIXTURE. HEAT A SKILLET TO MEDIUM AND BROWN QUESADILLAS ON BOTH SIDES. PLACE ON A COOKIE SHEET IN WARM OVEN WHILE BROWNING THE REMAINDER. CUT EACH QUESADILLA INTO 3 TRIANGULAR WEDGES. SERVE WARM. SERVES 6.

'TIS A SMALL MIND THAT CAN ONLY SPELL A WORD ONE WAY.

PICTURED ON OVERLEAF

EL GRANDO CHICKEN QUESADILLAS
    - PAGE 29

MOLDED SHRIMP DIP

MAKE AHEAD - SERVE WITH CRACKERS - AND RELAX!

10-OZ. CAN TOMATO SOUP	284 g
8 OZ. CREAM CHEESE, SOFTENED	250 g
7-OZ. CAN BROKEN SHRIMP, DRAINED	200 g
½ CUP FINELY CHOPPED ONION	125 mL
1 CUP FINELY CHOPPED CELERY	250 mL
1½ TBSP. GELATIN DISSOLVED IN	22 mL
½ CUP HOT WATER	125 mL

IN A SMALL PAN, HEAT SOUP UNTIL MELTED. BEAT IN CREAM CHEESE UNTIL SMOOTH. ADD REMAINING INGREDIENTS AND STIR. POUR INTO A GREASED 2-CUP MOLD. REFRIGERATE UNTIL SET.

DEBATE: WHAT'S IN DE MOUSETRAP

STILTON PÂTÉ

A FAVE!! SERVE WITH CRUSTY BREAD OR CRACKERS.

8 OZ. STILTON CHEESE	250 g
¼ CUP BUTTER	60 mL
4 OZ. CREAM CHEESE	125 g
2 TBSP. BRANDY	30 mL
FRESHLY GROUND PEPPER TO TASTE	

BRING STILTON, BUTTER AND CREAM CHEESE TO ROOM TEMPERATURE. ADD ALL INGREDIENTS TO FOOD PROCESSOR AND MIX. PLACE IN SMALL BOWL AND REFRIGERATE UNTIL SERVING TIME.

ZUCCHINI SQUARES

A GOOD MAKE-AHEAD - FREEZES WELL.

4 EGGS
4 SMALL ZUCCHINI, UNPEELED AND THINLY SLICED
1 CUP BISCUIT MIX   250 mL
1 MEDIUM ONION, FINELY CHOPPED
½ CUP FRESHLY GRATED   125 mL
        PARMESAN CHEESE
½ TSP. OREGANO   2 mL
1 TBSP. PARSLEY   15 mL
½ TSP. SEASONED SALT   2 mL
PEPPER TO TASTE
1 GARLIC CLOVE, MINCED
½ CUP VEGETABLE OIL   125 mL

PREHEAT OVEN TO 350°F. IN A LARGE BOWL, BEAT
EGGS. ADD REMAINING INGREDIENTS AND MIX
WELL. SPREAD IN GREASED 9" X 9" PAN. BAKE
35-40 MINUTES, OR UNTIL LIGHTLY BROWNED. CUT
INTO SQUARES.

WHERE THERE'S SMOKE, THERE'S TOAST.

SWISS BACON PLEASERS

8-OZ. PKG. REFRIGERATED
        CRESCENT ROLLS   250 g
4 SLICES SWISS CHEESE
3 EGGS, SLIGHTLY BEATEN
¾ CUP MILK   175 mL
1 TBSP. DICED ONION   15 mL
6 SLICES BACON, COOKED CRISP & CRUMBLED
1 TBSP. PARSLEY   15 mL

SWISS BACON PLEASERS

THIS RECIPE CONTINUED FROM PAGE 38.

PREHEAT OVEN TO 425°F. GREASE AND FLOUR 2 8"x 8" PANS. (A 9"x 13" PAN DOESN'T WORK!) SEPARATE ROLLS INTO RECTANGLES AND PRESS OVER BOTTOM AND SIDES OF EACH PAN. PLACE 2 CHEESE SLICES ON TOP OF DOUGH. COMBINE EGGS, MILK AND ONION. POUR ½ MIXTURE IN EACH PAN AND SPRINKLE WITH BACON AND PARSLEY. BAKE 15-18 MINUTES AND CUT INTO SQUARES. SERVE IMMEDIATELY.

SIGN OVER THE SCALES AT AN EXERCISE CLUB: "PRETEND IT'S YOUR I.Q."

WONTON CRISPIES

ADDICTIVE - YOU'LL WANT TO DOUBLE THIS!

¼ CUP MARGARINE	60 mL
20 WONTON WRAPPERS	
¼ CUP PARMESAN CHEESE	60 mL

MELT MARGARINE AND BRUSH SOME ON AN EDGED BAKING SHEET. CUT EACH WONTON DIAGONALLY TO MAKE TRIANGLES. PLACE CLOSE TOGETHER AND BRUSH TOPS WITH MARGARINE. SPRINKLE WITH CHEESE. BAKE AT 375°F. FOR 5 MINUTES. REPEAT UNTIL ALL ARE BAKED. IF YOU'RE INTO EXPERIMENTING, ADD HERBS OR CHOPPED GREEN ONIONS TO THE CHEESE. MAKES 40.

CHARRED PEPPER & FETA DIP

MAKE THIS THE DAY BEFORE YOU NEED IT!

3 LARGE RED PEPPERS
6 OZ. FETA CHEESE   170 g
2 TBSP. PINE NUTS   30 mL
1 TBSP. OLIVE OIL   15 mL

CUT PEPPERS IN HALF AND REMOVE SEEDS.
PLACE CUT-SIDE DOWN ON COOKIE SHEET. BROIL
UNTIL SKINS ARE BLACKENED AND PUFFED. PUT
PEPPERS IN PLASTIC BAG AND LET STAND FOR 10
MINUTES TO STEAM. REMOVE AND PEEL. PLACE
ALL INGREDIENTS IN FOOD PROCESSOR AND
BLEND. SERVE WITH WATER BISCUITS OR
UNSALTED CRACKERS OR FRESH VEGETABLES

I DON'T REALLY MIND THE FACT THAT MY SON IS
EARNING MORE MONEY THAN I DID ON MY FIRST JOB.
WHAT DOES DISTURB ME IS THAT HE'S 6 YEARS OLD
AND IT'S HIS ALLOWANCE.

SERVE THIS DELICIOUS GREEK DIP WITH PITA BREAD. ALSO TASTES GREAT WITH SOUVLAKI (PG. 158).

1 LONG ENGLISH CUCUMBER	
3 GARLIC CLOVES, MINCED	
2 TSP. SALT	10 mL
2 CUPS PLAIN SKIM MILK YOGURT	500 mL
1 CUP 7% SOUR CREAM	250 mL
1 TBSP. FINELY CHOPPED FRESH PARSLEY	15 mL
1/4 TSP. PEPPER	1 mL

GRATE CUCUMBER AND PLACE IN COLANDER. LET DRAIN FOR AT LEAST 1 HOUR. SQUEEZE OUT EXCESS LIQUID FROM CUCUMBER. COMBINE GARLIC, SALT, YOGURT, SOUR CREAM, PARSLEY AND PEPPER. ADD CUCUMBER TO YOGURT MIXTURE AND STIR WELL. CHILL BEFORE SERVING.

— FOR LESS THAN 1 GRAM FAT, SERVE 2 TBSP. WITH PITA WEDGE.

IF IT'S TRUE THAT TIME HEALS ALL WOUNDS, HOW COME WE DON'T GET BETTER WAITING IN THE DOCTOR'S OFFICE?

TAPENADE

"POOR MAN'S CAVIAR" - A GUTSY SPREAD FROM PROVENCE.

14-oz. CAN PITTED BLACK OLIVES, DRAINED	398 mL
1 LARGE GARLIC CLOVE, MINCED	
4-6 ANCHOVY FILLETS	
1 TBSP. CAPERS	15 mL
3 TBSP. LEMON JUICE	45 mL
1 BAGUETTE	

COMBINE ALL INGREDIENTS, EXCEPT BAGUETTE, IN FOOD PROCESSOR AND BLEND UNTIL FINELY MINCED. SERVE AT ROOM TEMPERATURE WITH TOASTED BAGUETTE SLICES.

FOR VARIETY: SPREAD BAGUETTE SLICES WITH GOAT CHEESE (CHÈVRE) AND TOP WITH THE TAPENADE. ALSO A GREAT DIP FOR FRESH VEGETABLES.

BY THE TIME A MAN REALIZES THAT MAYBE HIS FATHER WAS RIGHT, HE USUALLY HAS A SON WHO THINKS HE'S WRONG.

Jezebel

SO BE TEMPTED!

1 CUP PINEAPPLE JAM	250 mL
1¼ CUPS CRABAPPLE JELLY	300 mL
¼ CUP HORSERADISH	60 mL
1 TBSP. DRY MUSTARD	15 mL
8 OZ. LOW-FAT CREAM CHEESE	250 g

MIX JAM, JELLY, HORSERADISH AND DRY MUSTARD TOGETHER. PLACE IN REFRIGERATOR FOR AT LEAST 4 HOURS. SERVE WITH CREAM CHEESE AND MELBA TOAST. THE LEFTOVER MIXTURE KEEPS WELL IN THE REFRIGERATOR.

1.3 GRAMS FAT, SERVED WITH 1 TSP. LOW-FAT CREAM CHEESE ON MELBA TOAST.

WHERE THERE'S A WILL, THERE'S A RELATIVE.

CURRIED CHUTNEY SPREAD

2 - 8-OZ. PKG. CREAM CHEESE, ROOM TEMPERATURE	2 - 250 g
½ CUP MANGO OR RHUBARB CHUTNEY	125 mL
½ CUP CHOPPED ALMONDS, TOASTED	125 mL
1 TSP. CURRY	5 mL
½ TSP. DRY MUSTARD	2 mL

MIX ALL INGREDIENTS TOGETHER. CHILL. SERVE WITH CRACKERS OR USE TO STUFF CELERY. MAKES 3 CUPS.

HOT PEPPER ORANGE CHUTNEY

ALL YOU NEED IS SOME CRACKERS AND CREAM CHEESE AND YOU HAVE A NICE TANGY APPETIZER. GIFTABLE!

8 LARGE ORANGES	
3 CUPS CHOPPED RED PEPPER	750 mL
½ CUP CHOPPED JALAPEÑO PEPPERS	125 mL
1 CUP CHOPPED ONION	250 mL
1 CUP RAISINS	250 mL
1 CUP MIXED GLACE PEEL	250 mL
1½ CUPS WHITE WINE VINEGAR	375 mL
2 CUPS BROWN SUGAR	500 mL
¼ TSP. CAYENNE PEPPER	1 mL
1 TSP. CINNAMON	5 mL
½ TSP. NUTMEG	2 mL

PEEL ALL BUT 3 ORANGES. SLICE THE 3 UNPEELED ORANGES THINLY AND CUT EACH SLICE IN HALF. CUT PEELED ORANGES IN ½" CHUNKS. PLACE ALL INGREDIENTS IN A LARGE POT OVER MEDIUM-HIGH HEAT AND BRING TO A BOIL. REDUCE HEAT AND SIMMER UNTIL THICKENED. POUR INTO 8-OZ. JARS AND SEAL. PROCESS IN BOILING WATER 10 MINUTES. MAKES 12 JARS.

LESS THAN 1.5 GRAMS FAT SERVED WITH 1 TSP. LOW-FAT CREAM CHEESE ON MELBA TOAST.

43% OF ALL STATISTICS ARE WORTHLESS.

FIESTA CHICKEN TORTILLA SALAD

A DELICIOUS DINNER SALAD FOR 2 - ¡MUY SABROSO! - DON'T BE SHY, USE YOUR FINGERS FOR THE TORTILLA STRIPS.

1 WHOLE BONELESS, SKINLESS CHICKEN BREAST	
1 TBSP. TABASCO	15 mL
VEGETABLE OIL FOR FRYING	
3 SOFT CORN TORTILLAS, CUT IN 1/4" STRIPS	
SALT	
1/2 RED BELL PEPPER, CUT IN STRIPS	
4 CUPS ROMAINE LETTUCE, SLICED IN STRIPS	1 L

DRESSING

4 TBSP. TOASTED SESAME SEEDS	60 mL
2 TBSP. WHITE WINE VINEGAR	30 mL
1 TBSP. DIJON MUSTARD	15 mL
1/2 CUP VEGETABLE OIL	125 mL
SALT AND PEPPER TO TASTE	

TO PREPARE CHICKEN: CUT CHICKEN BREAST INTO 1/4" STRIPS AND TOSS WITH THE TABASCO. HEAT OIL (1/4" DEEP) UNTIL HOT IN HEAVY SKILLET. FRY TORTILLA STRIPS QUICKLY UNTIL GOLDEN. SET ON PAPER TOWEL TO DRAIN. SEASON WITH SALT. POUR OFF ALL BUT A LITTLE OIL AND SAUTÉ CHICKEN FOR 2-3 MINUTES. SET ASIDE.

TO PREPARE DRESSING: COMBINE INGREDIENTS IN BLENDER AND BLEND UNTIL SMOOTH.

TO PREPARE SALAD: PLACE LETTUCE, PEPPERS AND CHICKEN IN A BOWL AND TOSS WITH DRESSING. SERVE ON INDIVIDUAL PLATES AND ARRANGE TORTILLA STRIPS ON TOP. (PICTURED ON PAGE 53.)

BARBECUED THAI CHICKEN WITH ORIENTAL DRESSING

SERVE WITH SAVORY CHEDDAR BISCUITS (PAGE 26).

MARINADE

8 GARLIC CLOVES, CHOPPED	
3 TBSP. SOY SAUCE	45 mL
2 TSP. 5-SPICE POWDER	10 mL
1 TSP. HOT RED CHILI FLAKES	5 mL
1 TBSP. BROWN SUGAR	15 mL
½ TSP. SALT	2 mL
½ CUP CHOPPED CILANTRO	125 mL
⅓ CUP SHREDDED COCONUT (OPTIONAL)	75 mL

2 WHOLE BONELESS, SKINLESS CHICKEN BREASTS

ORIENTAL DRESSING

2 TBSP. RICE OR WHITE VINEGAR	30 mL
1 TBSP. VEGETABLE OIL	15 mL
1 TBSP. SESAME OIL	15 mL
2 TBSP. SOY SAUCE	30 mL
½ TSP. DRY MUSTARD	2 mL
½ TSP. SUGAR	2 mL
2 TSP. FINELY MINCED GINGER	10 mL
1 GARLIC CLOVE, MINCED	
1 TBSP. DICED GREEN ONION	15 mL
TOASTED SESAME SEEDS (OPTIONAL)	

SALAD GREENS: ROMAINE, ENDIVE, RADICCHIO (OFTEN SOLD IN MIXED PKGS.)

THE BEST WAY TO TELL A WOMAN'S AGE IS IN A VERY LOW VOICE.

BARBECUED THAI CHICKEN
WITH ORIENTAL DRESSING

THIS RECIPE CONTINUED FROM PAGE 46.

TO MAKE MARINADE: COMBINE ALL INGREDIENTS AND MARINATE CHICKEN OVERNIGHT IN REFRIGERATOR.

TO MAKE DRESSING: COMBINE INGREDIENTS IN A JAR AND SHAKE VIGOROUSLY.

GRILL CHICKEN OVER LOW HEAT ABOUT 5 MINUTES PER SIDE. CUT IN STRIPS AND SET ASIDE. TOSS SALAD GREENS WITH DRESSING AND PLACE CHICKEN STRIPS ON TOP. SPRINKLE SESAME SEEDS OVER ALL. SERVES 6.

7.5 GRAMS FAT PER SERVING (DOES NOT INCLUDE COCONUT AND SESAME SEEDS.)

DOCTOR TO OVERWEIGHT PATIENT: "YOU'LL HAVE TO GIVE UP THOSE INTIMATE DINNERS FOR TWO UNLESS YOU HAVE ANOTHER PERSON WITH YOU."

GRILLED CHICKEN AND SPINACH SALAD

A REFRESHING ENTRÉE TO SERVE ON A WARM SUMMER EVENING. HEAT UP THE GRILL INSTEAD OF YOUR KITCHEN.

SALAD

2 LBS. FRESH SPINACH, TORN	1 kg
1 WEDGE RED CABBAGE, THINLY SLICED	
8 THIN SLICES RED ONION	
1 LARGE ORANGE, PEELED AND SECTIONED	
4 BONELESS, SKINLESS CHICKEN BREAST HALVES	

DRESSING

¼ TSP. GRATED ORANGE PEEL	1 mL
1 TBSP. SOY SAUCE	15 mL
¼ TSP. FRESHLY GROUND PEPPER	1 mL
1 TSP. SUGAR	5 mL
3 TBSP. BRANDY	45 mL
3 TBSP. RED WINE VINEGAR	45 mL
2 SLICES BACON	
3 TBSP. VEGETABLE OIL	45 mL

HEAT BARBECUE. TOSS SPINACH, CABBAGE, ONION AND ORANGE IN A LARGE BOWL. SET ASIDE. GRILL CHICKEN OVER MEDIUM HEAT, 4 MINUTES PER SIDE. COOL SLIGHTLY.

TO PREPARE DRESSING: WHISK ORANGE PEEL, SOY SAUCE, PEPPER, SUGAR, BRANDY AND VINEGAR IN A CUP. SET ASIDE. COOK BACON UNTIL CRISP, DRAIN OFF ALL BUT 1 TBSP. OF THE DRIPPINGS. ADD VINEGAR MIXTURE AND COOK, STIRRING, ABOUT 45 SECONDS. REMOVE FROM HEAT.

GRILLED CHICKEN AND SPINACH SALAD

THIS RECIPE CONTINUED FROM PAGE 48.

WHISK IN OIL. POUR OVER SALAD AND TOSS TO COAT GREENS. DIVIDE SALAD AMONG 4 DINNER PLATES, TOP WITH CRUMBLED BACON. THINLY SLICE EACH CHICKEN BREAST AND FAN OVER EACH SERVING. SERVE WITH BRUSCHETTA ("ACES" PAGE 31) OR FOCACCIA (PAGE 24).

ROASTED RED PEPPER SALAD

2 LARGE RED PEPPERS, HALVED AND SEEDED
4 OZ. FETA CHEESE   115 g
FRESH BASIL LEAVES

DRESSING

2 GARLIC CLOVES, CRUSHED
1 TBSP. MINCED GINGER   15 mL
1/4 CUP OLIVE OIL   60 mL
1 TBSP. SESAME OIL   15 mL
GROUND PEPPER

BLACKEN PEPPER HALVES UNDER BROILER. PLACE IN BAG TO STEAM. PEEL PEPPERS. SLICE IN STRIPS AND ARRANGE ON PLATE WITH CRUMBLED FETA CHEESE AND BASIL LEAVES. SAUTÉ GARLIC AND GINGER IN OIL. COOL AND POUR OVER PEPPERS. SERVE WITH FRESHLY GROUND PEPPER. GREAT WITH STEAK. SERVES 4.

CHICKEN CAESAR SALAD WITH JALAPEÑO LIME DRESSING

A SOUTHWESTERN CAESAR FROM A CULINARY COUSIN. SERVE WITH TEXAS TOAST (PAGE 25).

MARINADE

¼ CUP VEGETABLE OIL	60 mL
JUICE OF 1 LIME	
1 GARLIC CLOVE, MINCED	
FRESHLY GROUND PEPPER	

4 BONELESS, SKINLESS CHICKEN BREAST HALVES

DRESSING

½ JALAPEÑO PEPPER	
1-2 GARLIC CLOVES, MINCED	
1 EGG YOLK	
1 TSP. DIJON MUSTARD	5 mL
2 ANCHOVY FILLETS, FINELY CHOPPED OR 2 TSP. (10 mL) ANCHOVY PASTE	
½ TSP. TABASCO SAUCE	2 mL
JUICE OF 1 LIME	
1 TBSP. BALSAMIC VINEGAR	15 mL
¼ TSP. CUMIN	1 mL
¾ CUP OLIVE OIL	175 mL

1 HEAD ROMAINE LETTUCE, WASHED, DRIED, TORN INTO BITE-SIZED PIECES	
½ CUP FRESHLY GRATED PARMESAN CHEESE	125 mL

IF DIAMONDS ARE A GIRL'S BEST FRIEND, WHY DOES A MAN HAVE TO SETTLE FOR A DOG?

CHICKEN CAESAR SALAD WITH JALAPEÑO LIME DRESSING

THIS RECIPE CONTINUED FROM PAGE 50.

TO PREPARE MARINADE AND CHICKEN: COMBINE MARINADE INGREDIENTS, ADD CHICKEN AND MARINATE AT ROOM TEMPERATURE FOR ½ HOUR. GRILL OR BROIL 3 MINUTES EACH SIDE. COOL AND CUT IN STRIPS.

TO PREPARE DRESSING: CHAR THE JALAPEÑO PEPPER IN A HEAVY SKILLET OVER MEDIUM-HIGH HEAT. TURN FREQUENTLY UNTIL BLACKENED. COOL, PEEL, SEED AND CHOP. PUT THIS AND REMAINING INGREDIENTS IN BLENDER AND BLEND UNTIL SMOOTH.

TOSS DRESSING WITH LETTUCE AND PARMESAN CHEESE. ARRANGE ON SALAD PLATES AND TOP WITH CHICKEN.

"WHAT'S YOUR DOG'S NAME?"

"WE CALL HIM BEN HUR. HE WAS JUST PLAIN OLD BEN UNTIL HE HAD PUPPIES"

CURRIED RICE SALAD

MAKE THE NIGHT BEFORE AND SERVE WITH SALMON OR HAM.

2 TBSP. CURRY POWDER	30 mL
2 TSP. MARGARINE	10 mL
3 CUPS CHICKEN BROTH	750 mL
1½ CUPS UNCOOKED RICE	375 mL
4 GREEN ONIONS, CHOPPED	
1½ TBSP. LEMON JUICE	22 mL
1 CUP LOW-FAT MAYONNAISE	250 mL
2 TBSP. MILK	30 mL
1 CUP CHOPPED APPLE	250 mL
½ CUP RAISINS	125 mL
¼ CUP SLIVERED ALMONDS, TOASTED	60 mL

IN A MEDIUM SAUCEPAN, SAUTÉ CURRY IN MARGARINE. STIR IN CHICKEN BROTH AND BRING TO BOIL. ADD RICE; COVER AND SIMMER 20 MINUTES, OR UNTIL ALL LIQUID IS ABSORBED. STIR IN GREEN ONION AND LEMON JUICE. CHILL THOROUGHLY. COMBINE MAYONNAISE AND MILK, BLEND WELL AND STIR INTO RICE MIXTURE WITH APPLES, RAISINS AND ALMONDS.

IT SELDOM OCCURS TO TEENAGERS THAT SOMEDAY THEY WILL KNOW AS LITTLE AS THEIR PARENTS.

PICTURED ON OVERLEAF

FIESTA CHICKEN TORTILLA SALAD
    - PAGE 45

SEAFOOD SALAD WITH TARRAGON MUSTARD DRESSING

THE DRESSING IS MAHVALOUS!!

DRESSING

1 LARGE EGG	
1 TBSP. DIJON MUSTARD	15 mL
2 TBSP. TARRAGON WINE VINEGAR	30 mL
1-2 TSP. TARRAGON	5-10 mL
SALT AND PEPPER TO TASTE	
1¼ CUPS VEGETABLE OIL	300 mL

SALAD

5 LARGE SHRIMP PER PERSON, SHELLED AND DEVEINED (FROZEN ARE FINE)	
3 SCALLOPS PER PERSON, QUARTERED IF LARGE	
1-1½ CUPS FROZEN PEAS	250-375 mL
6 GREEN ONIONS, CHOPPED	
SALT AND FRESHLY GROUND PEPPER TO TASTE	
ROMAINE LETTUCE, COARSELY TORN	

USING A FOOD PROCESSOR, BLEND TOGETHER EGG, MUSTARD, VINEGAR AND SEASONINGS. WITH MACHINE RUNNING, DRIZZLE IN OIL. MIXTURE WILL BE THICK AND SHINY.

TO PREPARE SALAD: IN A LARGE POT OF BOILING WATER, COOK SHRIMP FOR 1 MINUTE. ADD SCALLOPS. COOK 2 MINUTES, OR JUST UNTIL WATER RETURNS TO BOIL. DRAIN AND COOL UNDER COLD RUNNING WATER. RESERVE A FEW SHRIMP FOR GARNISH AND TOSS REMAINING WITH PEAS AND GREEN ONION. SEASON LIGHTLY AND TOSS WITH DESIRED AMOUNT OF DRESSING. PLACE ROMAINE ON INDIVIDUAL PLATES AND TOP WITH SHRIMP MIXTURE. SERVE WITH ADDITIONAL DRESSING ON THE SIDE.

PICKLED CITRUS SHRIMP SALAD

A REFRESHING MAIN DISH SALAD FOR 4.

MARINADE

1/3 CUP VEGETABLE OIL	75 mL
1/3 CUP LEMON JUICE	75 mL
1/3 CUP LIME JUICE	75 mL
3 TBSP. HONEY	45 mL
2 TBSP. CAPERS	30 mL
1 TSP. CELERY SEED	5 mL
1 TBSP. HORSERADISH	15 mL
1 TSP. TABASCO SAUCE	5 mL
1/2 TSP. SALT	2 mL

1 POUND LARGE SHRIMP, PEELED AND DEVEINED	500 g
1 LARGE ORANGE	
1 SMALL GRAPEFRUIT	
1 LARGE RED ONION, THINLY SLICED	
BIBB OR BUTTER LETTUCE LEAVES	

COMBINE MARINADE INGREDIENTS IN A LARGE BOWL. WHISK THOROUGHLY TO COMBINE. BLANCH SHRIMP FOR 1 MINUTE IN BOILING WATER, DRAIN AND ADD TO MARINADE. TOSS TO COAT. PEEL ORANGE AND GRAPEFRUIT, SCRAPING OFF WHITE PITH. (WHAT?) SEPARATE SECTIONS AND REMOVE SEEDS. ADD SECTIONS TO MARINADE ALONG WITH ONION. COVER AND REFRIGERATE OVERNIGHT, TOSSING OCCASIONALLY. SERVE ON A BED OF BIBB OR BUTTER LETTUCE AND DRIZZLE WITH A LITTLE MARINADE.

A FOOL AND HIS MONEY ARE INVITED PLACES.

SHOW-OFF TORTELLINI SALAD

You'll be a hit at the next pot luck. Hope the other people bring their share.

12-oz. pkg. herb tortellini with cheese	350 g
12-oz. pkg. spinach tortellini with cheese	350 g
2 cups broccoli florets	500 mL
14-oz. can artichoke hearts, quartered	398 mL
12-oz. pitted black olives, sliced	341 mL
1 lb. shrimp, cooked and tails removed	500 g
16-oz. bottle golden caesar dressing or spicy italian dressing	500 mL
2 cups halved cherry tomatoes	500 mL
1 cup freshly grated parmesan cheese	250 mL

Cook tortellini according to package directions. Drain well. In a large bowl, toss tortellini, broccoli, artichokes, olives and shrimp with dressing. Marinate overnight in refrigerator. Prior to serving, toss with tomatoes and parmesan cheese. Serves 8.

Reporter: Brzinlatowskiczinia is the name of the guy who was struck by lightning.

Editor: What was his name before he was struck?

FRENCH POTATO SALAD

2 LBS. SMALL RED NEW POTATOES	1 kg
5 STRIPS BACON, COOKED CRISP AND CHOPPED	
3 TBSP. CHOPPED FRESH PARSLEY	45 mL
2 TBSP. CHOPPED FRESH DILL OR	30 mL
2 TSP. (10 mL) DRIED	
4 GREEN ONIONS, CHOPPED	
1/3 CUP FINELY CHOPPED RED ONION	75 mL

DRESSING

1/3 CUP RED WINE VINEGAR	75 mL
3/4 CUP OLIVE OIL	175 mL
2 TSP. DIJON MUSTARD	10 mL
1 GARLIC CLOVE, MINCED	
FRESHLY GROUND BLACK PEPPER	

BOIL POTATOES UNTIL JUST TENDER. DRAIN AND CUT IN CHUNKS. PLACE IN SALAD BOWL WITH REMAINING SALAD INGREDIENTS. COMBINE DRESSING INGREDIENTS, MIX WELL AND TOSS WITH WARM POTATOES. ADD FRESHLY GROUND PEPPER. SALAD SHOULD MARINATE IN DRESSING FOR SEVERAL HOURS IN REFRIGERATOR. SERVES 6.

SUCCESS IS SOMETHING THAT ALWAYS SEEMS TO COME FASTER TO THE PERSON YOUR WIFE ALMOST MARRIED.

GREEN BEAN AND ROASTED ONION SALAD

THE NEW BUFFET SALAD - CARAMELIZED ONIONS ARE WORTH CRYING FOR!

DRESSING

1 CUP OLIVE OIL	250 mL
6 TBSP. BALSAMIC VINEGAR	90 mL
2 GARLIC CLOVES, MINCED	
½ TSP. SUGAR	2 mL
SALT AND PEPPER TO TASTE	

SALAD

1½ LBS. FRESH YOUNG GREEN BEANS, ENDS TRIMMED	750 g
3 LARGE RED ONIONS	
2 TBSP. OLIVE OIL	30 mL
SALT AND PEPPER TO TASTE	
2 TSP. SUGAR	10 mL
⅓ CUP TOASTED PINE NUTS	75 mL

WHISK ALL DRESSING INGREDIENTS TOGETHER AND SET ASIDE. PREHEAT OVEN TO 400°F. COOK BEANS UNTIL TENDER-CRISP. DRAIN AND PLUNGE INTO COLD WATER. CUT EACH ONION IN 8 WEDGES AND SEPARATE. SPRINKLE WITH OIL, SALT, PEPPER AND SUGAR. SPREAD ON AN EDGED BAKING SHEET AND BAKE FOR 30 MINUTES, STIRRING OCCASIONALLY, UNTIL BROWN AND CARAMELIZED. TOSS GREEN BEANS, ONIONS, AND DRESSING TOGETHER AND MARINATE FOR 3 HOURS IN THE REFRIGERATOR. MIX IN PINE NUTS JUST BEFORE SERVING.

SANTA FE SALAD

DRESSING

¼ CUP OLIVE OIL	60 mL
JUICE OF 2 LIMES	
¼ CUP CHOPPED CILANTRO	60 mL
1 TSP. CUMIN	5 mL
SALT AND FRESHLY GROUND PEPPER TO TASTE	

SALAD

19-OZ. CAN BLACK BEANS	540 mL
(TURTLE BEANS), RINSED AND DRAINED	
1 RED BELL PEPPER, DICED	
12-OZ. CAN KERNEL CORN, DRAINED	341 mL
⅓ CUP CHOPPED RED ONION	75 mL
1 JALAPEÑO PEPPER, SEEDED AND MINCED	

IN MEDIUM BOWL, WHISK TOGETHER OIL AND LIME JUICE. ADD CILANTRO, CUMIN, SALT AND PEPPER AND MIX WELL. STIR IN SALAD INGREDIENTS AND CORRECT SEASONING. SERVE AT ROOM TEMPERATURE WITH MUFFULETTA (PAGE 13) SERVES 6. (PICTURED ON PAGE 71.)

9.7 GRAMS OF FAT PER SERVING

A GARDEN IS A THING OF BEAUTY AND A JOB FOREVER.

WILD RICE SALAD

GOOD WITH GAME OR FOWL.

½ CUP WILD RICE	125 mL
1 CUP SEEDLESS GREEN GRAPES	250 mL
½ CUP PECANS, TOASTED	125 mL
1 RED PEPPER, CHOPPED	
4 GREEN ONIONS, CHOPPED	
½ CUP CHOPPED PARSLEY	125 mL

DRESSING

2 TBSP. OLIVE OIL	30 mL
2 TBSP. RED WINE VINEGAR	30 mL
2 TBSP. ORANGE JUICE	30 mL
GRATED RIND OF 1 ORANGE	
SALT & PEPPER TO TASTE	

COOK RICE AS PACKAGE DIRECTS. COOL. ADD
GRAPES, PECANS, PEPPER, ONIONS AND PARSLEY.
MIX DRESSING INGREDIENTS AND TOSS WITH RICE
MIXTURE. REFRIGERATE. SERVES 6.

 11 GRAMS FAT PER SERVING

FATHER OF TEENAGE DAUGHTER ANSWERING PHONE:
"NO, THIS ISN'T DREAMBOAT. THIS IS THE SUPPLY SHIP."

WARM SPINACH SALAD WITH APPLES AND BRIE

THIS IS A WINNER!

4 LARGE GRANNY SMITH APPLES	
¼ CUP MAPLE SYRUP	60 mL
8 CUPS WASHED SPINACH LEAVES	2 L
½ LB. BRIE, CUT IN SMALL PIECES	250 g
½ CUP TOASTED PECANS	125 mL

DRESSING

¼ CUP APPLE CIDER OR APPLE JUICE	60 mL
3 TBSP. CIDER VINEGAR	45 mL
1 TSP. DIJON MUSTARD	5 mL
1 GARLIC CLOVE, MINCED	
¼ CUP OLIVE OIL	60 mL
SALT AND PEPPER TO TASTE	

PEEL AND CORE APPLES; CUT INTO ½" SLICES. ARRANGE ON BAKING SHEET AND BRUSH WITH SYRUP. BROIL UNTIL GOLDEN; TURN, BRUSH SYRUP ON OTHER SIDE AND BROIL. PLACE SPINACH IN LARGE BOWL. WHISK DRESSING INGREDIENTS TOGETHER IN A SMALL SAUCEPAN AND HEAT UNTIL SIMMERING. POUR OVER SPINACH, TOSS AND ADD CHEESE, APPLES AND NUTS. DEE-LISH!

IT'S COSTING ABOUT TWICE AS MUCH TO LIVE BEYOND YOUR MEANS AS IT DID TEN YEARS AGO.

STRAWBERRY AND CHÈVRE SALAD

WHEN NANNY (OR THE REST OF THE HERD) IS COMING FOR LUNCH. SERVE WITH BAGUETTE (PAGE 23) OR CROISSANTS AND A GLASS OF BUBBLY.

VINAIGRETTE

1 GARLIC CLOVE, MINCED	
½ TSP. HONEY DIJON MUSTARD	2 mL
2 TBSP. RASPBERRY VINEGAR	30 mL
1 TBSP. BALSAMIC VINEGAR	15 mL
1 TBSP. BROWN SUGAR	15 mL
¼ CUP VEGETABLE OIL	60 mL

SALAD

6 CUPS MIXED GREENS	1.5 L
½ CUP CRUMBLED CHÈVRE (GOAT CHEESE)	125 mL
- BRIE IS GOOD TOO	
¼ CUP SLIVERED ALMONDS, TOASTED	60 mL
2 CUPS HALVED STRAWBERRIES	500 mL
SALT AND FRESHLY GROUND PEPPER TO TASTE	

TO PREPARE VINAIGRETTE: IN A SMALL BOWL, COMBINE GARLIC, MUSTARD, VINEGARS AND BROWN SUGAR. WHISK IN OIL.

TO PREPARE SALAD: IN A LARGE BOWL, TOSS GREENS WITH VINAIGRETTE. PLACE AN EQUAL PORTION ON 4 SALAD PLATES. TOP WITH CHEESE, NUTS AND STRAWBERRIES. SPRINKLE WITH SALT AND PEPPER.

WHY DO SINGLE MEN LIVE LONGER THAN MARRIED MEN? BECAUSE THEY WANT TO.

FRUIT 'N' SPINACH SALAD

¼ CUP WHITE WINE VINEGAR	60 mL
2 TBSP. VEGETABLE OIL	30 mL
2 TBSP. HONEY	30 mL
1 TSP. POPPY SEEDS	5 mL
½ TSP. DRY MUSTARD	2 mL
8 CUPS TORN SPINACH	2 L
1 MEDIUM PAPAYA, PEELED AND CUBED	
OR 2 MEDIUM PEARS, PEELED AND CUBED	
1½ CUPS HALVED SEEDLESS GRAPES	375 mL

IN A JAR, COMBINE VINEGAR, OIL, HONEY, POPPY SEEDS AND DRY MUSTARD. COVER AND SHAKE WELL. COMBINE SPINACH, PAPAYA (OR PEARS) AND GRAPES. SHAKE DRESSING AGAIN AND POUR OVER SALAD. TOSS TO COAT AND SERVE IMMEDIATELY. SERVES 8.

 3.8 GRAMS OF FAT PER SERVING

"LINDA, WHY DO YOU WEAR TWO PAIRS OF SHORTS ON THE GOLF COURSE?"

"IN CASE I GET A HOLE IN ONE." AND SO SHE DID!

SALSA MOLD

A '90'S VERSION OF TOMATO ASPIC!

2 - 3-OZ. PKGS. LEMON JELLY POWDER	2 - 85 g
2 CUPS BOILING WATER	500 mL
1½ CUPS TOMATO JUICE	375 mL
1 CUP SALSA	250 mL

COMPLETELY DISSOLVE JELLY POWDER IN BOILING WATER. ADD TOMATO JUICE AND SALSA. MIX WELL AND POUR INTO A GREASED 5-CUP MOLD. REFRIGERATE AT LEAST 4 HOURS - UNTIL SET. SERVES 6.

0.8 GRAMS OF FAT PER SERVING

A BIRD IN THE HAND IS SAFER THAN ONE OVERHEAD.

BALSAMIC POPPY SEED DRESSING

2 TBSP. BALSAMIC VINEGAR	30 mL
2 TBSP. ORANGE JUICE	30 mL
1 TBSP. POPPY SEEDS	15 mL
1 TSP. SUGAR	5 mL
½ TSP. DRY MUSTARD	2 ML
¼ TSP. SALT	1 mL
2 TBSP. WHITE WINE	30 mL
2 TBSP. OIL	30 mL
1 GREEN ONION, MINCED	

COMBINE, SHAKE WELL AND DRIZZLE OVER GREEN SALAD.

2.6 GRAMS FAT PER 1 TBSP.

BALSAMIC VINAIGRETTE

DRIZZLE OVER A VARIETY OF GREENS: BIBB
LETTUCE, LEAF LETTUCE, ENDIVE, RADICCHIO,
ARUGULA (YOU CAN BUY THIS COMBO PACKAGED AT
MOST STORES).

⅓ CUP BALSAMIC VINEGAR	75 mL
¼ CUP OLIVE OIL	60 mL
¼ CUP DRY WHITE WINE	60 mL

JUICE OF 1 LIME
SALT AND FRESHLY GROUND PEPPER TO TASTE

POUR VINEGAR INTO A SMALL BOWL AND
GRADUALLY WHISK IN OIL. WHISK IN WINE AND
LIME JUICE, SEASON AND STORE IN
REFRIGERATOR. JUST BEFORE SERVING, SHAKE
WELL AND DRIZZLE OVER GREENS.

 4 GRAMS FAT IN 1 TBSP. DRESSING

DID YOU EVER STOP TO WONDER ABOUT PEOPLE WHO
SIT AROUND FOR HOURS DRINKING INSTANT COFFEE?

ITALIAN DRESSING

1 CUP OLIVE OIL	250 mL
¼ CUP WHITE WINE VINEGAR	60 mL
1 TBSP. FRESH LEMON JUICE	15 mL
¾ TSP. OREGANO	4 mL
½ TSP. DRY MUSTARD	2 mL
¼ TSP. THYME	1 mL
1 GARLIC CLOVE, MINCED	
1 TSP. MINCED ONION	5 mL
1 TSP. HONEY	5 mL
SALT AND PEPPER TO TASTE	

COMBINE ALL INGREDIENTS. BLENDERIZE AND STORE IN REFRIGERATOR. MAKES ABOUT 1½ CUPS.

IN SOME PARTS OF THE WORLD, PEOPLE PRAY IN THE STREETS. IN THIS COUNTRY THEY'RE CALLED PEDESTRIANS.

AN EXCELLENT COMPLEMENT TO CHICKEN AND SPINACH SALAD (PAGE 48).

2 CUPS FRESH RASPBERRIES OR	500 mL
2 - 10-OZ. PKGS. FROZEN (THAWED)	
1½ CUPS WATER, DIVIDED	375 mL
1 CUP CRANBERRY COCKTAIL	250 mL
¾ CUP SUGAR	175 mL
1 CINNAMON STICK	
3 WHOLE CLOVES	
1 TBSP. LEMON JUICE	15 mL
8 OZ. SKIM MILK RASPBERRY YOGURT	250 g
⅓ CUP LOW-FAT SOUR CREAM	75 mL
CINNAMON	

PUT RASPBERRIES AND ¼ CUP OF THE WATER IN BLENDER AND PURÉE UNTIL SMOOTH. IN LARGE SAUCEPAN COMBINE PURÉED FRUIT, REMAINING 1¼ CUPS WATER, CRANBERRY COCKTAIL, SUGAR, CINNAMON STICK AND CLOVES. COOK OVER MEDIUM HEAT UNTIL MIXTURE BEGINS TO BOIL; REMOVE FROM HEAT AND COOL. STRAIN SOUP INTO LARGE BOWL. ADD LEMON JUICE AND YOGURT; WHISK UNTIL WELL BLENDED. COVER AND REFRIGERATE UNTIL COLD. POUR INTO SERVING DISHES AND TOP EACH WITH SOUR CREAM AND A SPRINKLE OF CINNAMON.
SERVES 6.

1.6 GRAMS FAT PER SERVING

YOU KNOW YOU'RE GETTING OLDER WHEN HAPPY HOUR IS A NAP.

FRESH TOMATO SOUP WITH PESTO

THE VERY BEST THING TO DO WITH GARDEN FRESH TOMATOES.

PESTO SAUCE

2 GARLIC CLOVES, CHOPPED	
1 CUP FRESH BASIL	250 mL
¼ CUP FRESHLY GRATED PARMESAN CHEESE	60 mL
2 TBSP. PINE NUTS	30 mL
¼ CUP OLIVE OIL	60 mL

SOUP

8 LARGE FRESH TOMATOES	
⅓ CUP MINCED SHALLOTS	75 mL
2 TBSP. OLIVE OIL	30 mL
2 TSP. SALT	10 mL
2 TSP. SUGAR	10 mL
FRESHLY GROUND PEPPER TO TASTE	

TO MAKE PESTO SAUCE: COMBINE GARLIC, BASIL, PARMESAN AND NUTS IN A BLENDER AND PURÉE. WITH MACHINE RUNNING, SLOWLY ADD OIL UNTIL MIXTURE IS CONSISTENCY OF THICK MAYONNAISE. STORE IN JAR IN REFRIGERATOR. LEFTOVER SAUCE IS GOOD ON PASTA.

TO MAKE SOUP: POUR BOILING WATER OVER TOMATOES, LEAVE 2 MINUTES, DRAIN AND PLUNGE INTO COLD WATER. WHEN SKINS SPLIT, PEEL AND CHOP. SET ASIDE. SAUTÉ SHALLOTS IN OIL UNTIL SOFTENED. ADD CHOPPED TOMATOES AND SEASONINGS. SIMMER 15 MINUTES. TRANSFER TO FOOD PROCESSOR AND PURÉE UNTIL SMOOTH. HEAT. GARNISH EACH SERVING WITH 1 TBSP. PESTO SAUCE. SERVES 6.

— 6.6 GRAMS FAT PER SERVING

GARLIC SOUP

THIS IS THE CURE - THE FLAVOR IS MILD AND THE AROMA ENTICING.

¼ CUP BUTTER	60 mL
2 TBSP. OLIVE OIL	30 mL
3 LARGE ONIONS, SLICED	
2 HEADS OF GARLIC, CLOVES SEPARATED AND PEELED	
½ TSP. CUMIN	2 mL
½ TSP. DRY MUSTARD	2 mL
4-5 CUPS CHICKEN STOCK	1-1.25 L
1 CUP HALF AND HALF CREAM	250 mL
CHOPPED PARSLEY FOR GARNISH	

MELT BUTTER, ADD OIL AND SAUTÉ ONIONS AND GARLIC IN SAUCEPAN. COVER AND COOK GENTLY ON LOW HEAT FOR 1 HOUR, UNTIL MIXTURE IS VERY SOFT. ADD CUMIN AND MUSTARD WITH 2 CUPS OF CHICKEN STOCK AND SIMMER FOR 10 MINUTES. TRANSFER MIXTURE TO FOOD PROCESSOR AND PURÉE. RETURN MIXTURE TO SAUCEPAN AND ADD CREAM AND REMAINING CHICKEN STOCK TO DESIRED CONSISTENCY. HEAT GENTLY AND GARNISH WITH PARSLEY.

ALL HUSBANDS ARE ALIKE, BUT THEY HAVE DIFFERENT FACES SO YOU CAN TELL THEM APART.

PICTURED ON OVERLEAF

POTATO AND LEEK SOUP

SMOOTH AS A SWEET TALKIN' MAN!

1½ cups chopped leeks, (use white part only)	375 mL
½ cup chopped onions	125 mL
1 garlic clove, minced	
¼ cup margarine	60 mL
4 cups chicken broth	1 L
1½ cups peeled, diced raw potato	375 mL
1 cup whipping cream	250 mL
1 tsp. salt	5 mL
¼ tsp. pepper	1 mL
finely chopped green onions or chives	

Sauté leeks, onions and garlic in margarine until translucent. Add broth and potatoes; cook until tender. Purée mixture in blender or food processor. Add cream, salt and pepper. Chill at least 24 hours. Garnish with green onions or chives. Heat gently or serve cold. Serves 4-6.

YOUTH LOOKS FOR GREENER PASTURES; MIDDLE AGE IS WHEN WE CAN HARDLY MOW THE ONE WE'VE GOT.

SPRING BORSCH

THIS IS BABA'S WONDERFUL SOUP FOR FRESH NEW BEETS. THE PICKLING SPICE WILL GIVE YOUR KITCHEN A RICH AROMA.

10-12 MEDIUM BEETS, CUBED OR SHREDDED	
1 MEDIUM ONION, CHOPPED	
3-4 MEDIUM CARROTS, CHOPPED	
1 MEDIUM POTATO, PEELED AND CHOPPED	
1 SMALL CABBAGE, SHREDDED	
2 TBSP. FRESH CHOPPED DILL	30 mL
1 TBSP. PICKLING SPICE	15 mL
10-OZ. CAN TOMATO SOUP	284 mL
LOW-FAT SOUR CREAM FOR GARNISH	

PLACE VEGETABLES AND SPICES IN A 4-QUART DUTCH OVEN, COVER WITH WATER AND COOK UNTIL TENDER. (THE PICKLING SPICES CAN BE TIED IN A CHEESECLOTH OR PLACED IN A TEA LEAF HOLDER). ADD THE TOMATO SOUP. SERVE WITH 1 TBSP. OF SOUR CREAM. SERVES 6.

NOTE: IF THE BEETS ARE MATURE, COOK THEM IN THEIR SKINS, REMOVE AND COOL. POP OFF SKINS, CUBE OR SHRED AND ADD BACK TO THE SOUP.

—☼— 1.1 GRAMS FAT PER SERVING (DOES NOT INCLUDE SOUR CREAM.)

COMMON KNOWLEDGE IS A SOURCE CITED FOR A FACT YOU JUST MADE UP.

QUICK LENTIL SOUP

A NUTRITIOUS ANSWER TO THE WEEKDAY RUSH - COOK AND PREPARE THIS LOW-FAT SOUP IN LESS THAN AN HOUR.

2 ONIONS, CHOPPED	
1 GARLIC CLOVE, MINCED	
1 TBSP. OLIVE OIL	15 mL
½ TSP. GINGER	2 mL
½ TSP. PAPRIKA	2 mL
½ TSP. TURMERIC	2 mL
3 CUPS BEEF STOCK	750 mL
28-OZ. CAN TOMATOES, CHOPPED	796 mL
19-OZ. CAN LENTILS	540 mL
19-OZ. CAN CHICKPEAS, DRAINED	540 mL
¼ CUP CHOPPED FRESH BASIL OR	60 mL
1 TBSP. (15 mL) DRIED	
SALT AND PEPPER TO TASTE	

SAUTÉ ONIONS AND GARLIC IN OIL. STIR IN GINGER, PAPRIKA AND TURMERIC AND COOK 1 MINUTE. STIR IN BEEF STOCK AND TOMATOES, BRING TO BOIL AND SIMMER FOR 30 MINUTES. ADD REMAINING INGREDIENTS AND SIMMER 15 MINUTES MORE. MAKES ENOUGH FOR 6. FREEZES WELL.

 4.7 GRAMS FAT PER SERVING

TELEVISION HAS OPENED MANY DOORS - ESPECIALLY ON REFRIGERATORS.

MEXICAN BLACK BEAN SOUP

NUTRITIOUS - INEXPENSIVE - VEGETARIAN!!

2 CUPS DRIED BLACK (TURTLE) BEANS	500 mL
2 ONIONS, CHOPPED	
3 GARLIC CLOVES, MINCED	
2 STALKS CELERY, CHOPPED	
1 TBSP. OLIVE OIL	15 mL
2 TBSP. CHILI POWDER	30 mL
1 TSP. HOT PEPPER SAUCE	5 mL
1 JALAPEÑO, CHOPPED	
2 TSP. OREGANO	10 mL
1 TSP. CUMIN	5 mL
1 TSP. FENNEL SEEDS	5 mL
6 CUPS CHICKEN OR VEGETABLE STOCK	1.5 L
28-OZ. CAN STEWED TOMATOES	796 mL
4 TSP. FRESH LIME JUICE	20 mL
SALT & PEPPER	

GARNISH SOUR CREAM, CILANTRO OR LIME SLICE

IN LARGE POT COVER BEANS WITH 6 CUPS OF WATER - BRING TO BOIL AND COOK 2 MINUTES. REMOVE FROM HEAT; LET STAND 1 HOUR. DRAIN, RINSE AND DRAIN AGAIN. SAUTÉ ONIONS, GARLIC AND CELERY IN OIL UNTIL SOFTENED. STIR IN CHILI, HOT SAUCE, JALAPEÑO, OREGANO, CUMIN AND FENNEL. COOK FOR 1 MINUTE. ADD BEANS AND STOCK. SIMMER FOR 1½ HOURS, UNTIL BEANS ARE TENDER. ADD TOMATOES, LIME JUICE, SALT AND PEPPER; SIMMER FOR 10 MINUTES. PURÉE SOUP IN BATCHES - RETURN TO POT AND HEAT. SERVE WITH YOUR CHOICE OF GARNISH. IF SOUP IS TOO THICK, ADD MORE STOCK. SERVES 8.

3.7 GRAMS OF FAT PER SERVING (DOES NOT INCLUDE SOUR CREAM.)

A COLD WINTER'S NIGHT, HOMEMADE SOUP, A LOAF OF BREAD AND PERHAPS A VIDEO??

6 SLICES BACON, CHOPPED	
2 MEDIUM ONIONS, CHOPPED	
3 STALKS CELERY, CHOPPED	
3-4 GARLIC CLOVES, MINCED	
¼ TSP. EACH MARJORAM, THYME	1 mL
½ TSP. EACH OREGANO, ROSEMARY	2 mL
2 TBSP. CHOPPED FRESH BASIL	30 mL
OR 2 TSP. (10 mL) DRIED	
¼ CUP CHOPPED FRESH PARSLEY	60 mL
½ TSP. HOT RED PEPPER FLAKES	2 mL
5 CUPS CHICKEN STOCK	1.25 L
28-OZ. CAN ITALIAN TOMATOES,	798 mL
CHOPPED	
⅔ CUP BABY SHELL PASTA	150 mL
14-OZ. CAN ARTICHOKE HEARTS	398 mL
(12-14 COUNT), DRAINED AND CUT	
INTO WEDGES	
SALT AND PEPPER TO TASTE	
GRATED PARMESAN CHEESE TO SPRINKLE	

IN A LARGE HEAVY POT, COOK BACON, ONIONS, CELERY, GARLIC, HERBS AND HOT PEPPER FLAKES, UNTIL ONIONS ARE SOFTENED. STIR IN STOCK AND TOMATOES. BRING TO BOIL. ADD PASTA. REDUCE HEAT AND SIMMER, UNCOVERED, 10 MINUTES, OR UNTIL PASTA IS JUST TENDER. STIR IN ARTICHOKES AND SEASON TO TASTE. SERVE WITH A SPRINKLING OF PARMESAN CHEESE. SERVES 6.

4.9 GRAMS OF FAT PER SERVING

7.4 GRAMS OF FAT PER SERVING WITH 1 TBSP. PARMESAN CHEESE

GREAT FAMILY MEAL. DON'T FORGET THE CRUSTY BUNS.

1 MEDIUM ONION, CHOPPED	
2 STALKS CELERY, CHOPPED	
3 CARROTS, CHOPPED	
3 GARLIC CLOVES, MINCED	
1 TBSP. MARGARINE	15 mL
28-OZ. CAN TOMATOES, CHOPPED	796 mL
19-OZ. CAN TOMATOES, CHOPPED	540 mL
1½ TSP. SUGAR	7 mL
6 CUPS WATER	1.5 L
3 TBSP. CHICKEN BOUILLON POWDER	45 mL
2 TBSP. PARSLEY	30 mL
¼ CUP FRESH CHOPPED BASIL OR	60 mL
1½ TBSP. (22 mL) DRIED	
10-OZ. PKG. VEAL TORTELLINI,	300 g
FRESH OR FROZEN	
SALT AND PEPPER TO TASTE	

SAUTÉ ONION, CELERY, CARROTS AND GARLIC IN MELTED MARGARINE UNTIL TENDER-CRISP, ABOUT 5 MINUTES. IN A LARGE POT, ADD TOMATOES, SUGAR, WATER, CHICKEN BOUILLON, PARSLEY AND BASIL. ADD VEGGIES AND BRING TO A GENTLE BOIL. REDUCE HEAT AND SIMMER 1 HOUR. ADD TORTELLINI AND CONTINUE TO SIMMER UNTIL TORTELLINI IS COOKED (ABOUT 10 MINUTES). ADD SALT AND PEPPER TO TASTE. SERVES 8.

4.4 GRAMS OF FAT PER SERVING

JUST FOR THE HALIBUT - CHOWDER

FOR FISH AND WINE ... THIS IS DIVINE.

2 MEDIUM ONIONS, DICED	
3 CUPS SLICED MUSHROOMS	750 mL
2 LARGE RED PEPPERS, DICED	
2 TBSP. BUTTER	30 mL
1 TBSP. LEMON JUICE	15 mL
3 - 10-OZ. CANS CHICKEN BROTH	3 - 284 mL
3-4 MEDIUM NEW POTATOES, PEELED AND CUBED	
2 TBSP. CORNSTARCH	30 mL
2 TBSP. WATER	30 mL
1 LB. HALIBUT, CUT INTO BITE-SIZED PIECES	500 g
1/2 CUP MINCED PARSLEY	125 mL
1/2 CUP WHITE WINE OR VERMOUTH (OPTIONAL)	125 mL
1 CUP 7% SOUR CREAM	250 mL
SALT AND PEPPER TO TASTE	

SAUTÉ ONIONS, MUSHROOMS AND PEPPERS IN
BUTTER UNTIL TENDER. ADD LEMON JUICE, BROTH
AND POTATOES. BRING TO A BOIL, COVER AND
SIMMER UNTIL POTATOES ARE TENDER. BLEND
TOGETHER CORNSTARCH AND WATER AND ADD TO
MIXTURE. ADD FISH, PARSLEY AND WINE. COVER
AND SIMMER JUST UNTIL FISH FLAKES EASILY.
ADD SOUR CREAM AND SALT AND PEPPER.
SERVES 8.

9.2 GRAMS OF FAT PER SERVING

REAL WOMEN DON'T HAVE HOT FLASHES - THEY HAVE
POWER SURGES

CHICKEN SOUP WITH MATZO BALLS

MAZEL TOV!

2 EGGS	
1 EGG WHITE	
½ TSP. SALT	2 mL
¾ CUP MATZO MEAL	175 mL
1 TBSP. VEGETABLE OIL	15 mL
3 TBSP. COLD WATER	45 mL
8 CUPS CHICKEN BROTH	2 L
1 LARGE CARROT, CHOPPED	
⅓ CUP CHOPPED GREEN ONION	75 mL
1 CUP BROCCOLI FLORETS	250 mL
1 CUP SLICED MUSHROOMS	250 mL
2 TBSP. CHOPPED DILL OR PARSLEY	30 mL

WHISK TOGETHER EGGS, EGG WHITE AND SALT. WHISK IN MATZO MEAL, OIL AND WATER. COVER AND CHILL AT LEAST 1 HOUR OR OVERNIGHT. IN LARGE POT BRING CHICKEN BROTH TO A BOIL AND ADD CARROT AND ONION. REDUCE HEAT TO MEDIUM-LOW AND COOK 5 MINUTES. BARELY MOISTEN HANDS TO ROLL MATZO DOUGH INTO TEASPOON-SIZED BALLS (MAKES ABOUT 24 BALLS). DROP INTO SIMMERING BROTH. COOK, COVERED, FOR 15 MINUTES. DON'T PEEK! BROTH MUST SIMMER RAPIDLY TO ALLOW BALLS TO EXPAND PROPERLY. ADD BROCCOLI AND MUSHROOMS AND SIMMER UNTIL BROCCOLI IS JUST TENDER (2-3 MINUTES). SPRINKLE WITH DILL OR PARSLEY. SERVES 6.

 5.7 GRAMS OF FAT PER SERVING

CELEBRATE CHINESE NEW YEAR WITH THIS SAVORY SOUP.

3 - 10-OZ. CANS CHICKEN BROTH	3 - 284 mL
3 CUPS WATER	750 mL
1 TSP. SESAME OIL	5 mL
3 THIN SLICES FRESH GINGER	
1 CUP LEFTOVER RARE ROAST BEEF	250 mL
(OR COOKED SLICED CHICKEN), CUT IN STRIPS	
½ LB. RAW SHRIMP, PEELED & DEVEINED.	250 g
1-2 CUPS FRESH PEAPODS	250-500 mL
1 CUP THINLY CHOPPED CARROTS	250 mL
8-OZ. CAN SLICED WATER CHESTNUTS, DRAINED	227 mL
14-OZ. CAN BABY CORN, DRAINED	398 mL
3 STALKS BOK CHOY, CHOPPED	
4-OZ. PKG. FROZEN WONTONS	115 g
1 CUP THINLY SLICED GREEN ONIONS	250 mL

IN LARGE POT COMBINE BROTH, WATER, OIL AND GINGER. BRING TO BOIL. ADD REMAINING INGREDIENTS EXCEPT WONTONS & GREEN ONIONS. REDUCE HEAT AND SIMMER 12 MINUTES. MEANWHILE, COOK WONTONS ACCORDING TO PACKAGE DIRECTIONS. DRAIN, ADD WONTONS TO BROTH MIXTURE AND SPRINKLE WITH GREEN ONIONS. MAKES ENOUGH FOR 8 LARGE SERVINGS.

6.2 GRAMS FAT PER SERVING

BAD SPELLERS OF THE WORLD UNTIE.

BEEF VEGETABLE SOUP

THE SECRET TO GOOD SOUP IS TO SAUTÉ THE VEGGIES - YOU'VE GOT THE SECRET!

BEEF STOCK

3 LBS. BEEF SOUP BONES	1.5 kg
10 CUPS COLD WATER	2.5 L
6 PEPPERCORNS	
2 WHOLE CLOVES	
2 BAY LEAVES	
1/8 TSP. THYME	0.5 mL
1/4 TSP. MARJORAM	1 mL
1/2 CUP DICED CARROTS	125 mL
1/2 CUP DICED ONIONS	125 mL
1/2 CUP DICED CELERY	125 mL
1 TBSP. SALT	15 mL

SPREAD BONES IN ROASTING PAN AND BAKE AT 400°F FOR 1 HOUR, OR UNTIL BROWNED. THIS WILL ENHANCE THE FLAVOR OF YOUR SOUP. TRANSFER BONES TO STOCK POT AND ADD REMAINING INGREDIENTS. HEAT SLOWLY TO BOILING POINT THEN SIMMER FOR 3 HOURS OR MORE. SKIM OFF FAT FROM TIME TO TIME. REMOVE FROM HEAT AND STRAIN. COVER AND REFRIGERATE STOCK UNTIL COMPLETELY COLD. REMOVE ANY FAT FROM TOP. FREEZE IN SMALL CONTAINERS. MAKES APPROXIMATELY 6 CUPS OF STOCK. GOOD FOR STEWS, GRAVIES AND THE FOLLOWING WONDERFUL SOUP!

BEEF VEGETABLE SOUP

THIS RECIPE CONTINUED FROM PAGE 82.

THE SOUP

2 TBSP. MARGARINE OR VEGETABLE OIL	30 mL
1 CUP CHOPPED CARROTS	250 mL
1 CUP CHOPPED TURNIPS	250 mL
1 CUP CHOPPED CELERY	250 mL
1 CUP CHOPPED ONIONS	250 mL
1 CUP CHOPPED POTATOES	250 mL
1/4 CUP BARLEY	60 mL
5 CUPS BEEF STOCK	1.25 L
2 1/2 CUPS WATER	625 mL
SALT & PEPPER TO TASTE	
2 TBSP. FINELY CHOPPED PARSLEY	30 mL

MELT MARGARINE AND ADD ALL VEGETABLES
EXCEPT POTATOES TO STOCK POT. SAUTÉ
10 MINUTES, STIRRING CONSTANTLY. ADD POTATOES,
COVER AND SAUTÉ 2 MORE MINUTES. ADD BARLEY,
STOCK AND WATER AND BRING TO A BOIL. SIMMER
1 HOUR, OR UNTIL VEGETABLES ARE TENDER. ADD
MORE WATER IF NECESSARY. SEASON WITH SALT
AND PEPPER AND SPRINKLE WITH PARSLEY.
SERVES 8.

 6.2 GRAMS FAT PER SERVING

JURY OF PEERS: TWELVE PEOPLE WITH WEAK
BLADDERS.

BAKED MEDITERRANEAN VEGGIES

TASTY VEGGIES FOR YOUR CREW - AND DARN HEALTHY TOO!

1 SMALL EGGPLANT, CUT INTO 1" CUBES	
1 LARGE RED PEPPER, CUT INTO 1" PIECES	
1 MEDIUM ZUCCHINI, CUT INTO 1/2" SLICES	
1 SMALL RED ONION, CUT IN WEDGES	
2 GARLIC CLOVES, SLICED	
2 BAY LEAVES	
1 TSP. BASIL	5 mL
1 TSP. ROSEMARY	5 mL
SALT AND PEPPER TO TASTE	
2 TBSP. OLIVE OIL	30 mL
6-oz. JAR MARINATED ARTICHOKE HEARTS, DRAIN AND RESERVE MARINADE	184 mL

PREHEAT OVEN TO 400°F. IN A SHALLOW BAKING DISH, COMBINE VEGGIES WITH GARLIC, BAY LEAVES, BASIL, ROSEMARY, SALT AND PEPPER. DRIZZLE WITH OLIVE OIL AND RESERVED ARTICHOKE MARINADE. BAKE ABOUT 40 MINUTES STIRRING EVERY 10 MINUTES UNTIL VEGGIES ARE FORK-TENDER. CUT ARTICHOKE HEARTS INTO 1/2" PIECES AND STIR INTO VEGGIES. BAKE 5 MINUTES MORE AND DISCARD BAY LEAVES. SERVES 4.

 10.4 GRAMS FAT PER SERVING

HIRE A STUDENT WHILE THEY STILL KNOW EVERYTHING THERE IS TO KNOW.

ZUCCHINI-STUFFED TOMATOES

EASY AND COLORFUL.

3 MEDIUM ZUCCHINI, UNPEELED	
½ TSP. SALT	2 mL
4 LARGE FIRM TOMATOES	
¼ CUP MARGARINE	60 mL
1 MEDIUM ONION, CHOPPED	
1 GARLIC CLOVE, MINCED	
1 TBSP. BROWN SUGAR	15 mL
2 TBSP. GRATED PARMESAN CHEESE	30 mL
2 TBSP. MINCED FRESH PARSLEY	30 mL

GRATE ZUCCHINI COARSELY AND TOSS IN A BOWL WITH SALT. SET ASIDE FOR ABOUT 30 MINUTES. REMOVE STEMS AND CUT TOMATOES IN HALF HORIZONTALLY. REMOVE PULP, CHOP AND PLACE IN SMALL BOWL. PLACE TOMATO SHELLS CUT-SIDE DOWN AND DRAIN ON PAPER TOWELS. IN FRYING PAN, MELT MARGARINE AND SAUTÉ ONIONS AND GARLIC UNTIL TENDER. ADD TOMATO PULP. SIMMER TO EVAPORATE MOISTURE. REMOVE FRYING PAN FROM HEAT. DRAIN ALL LIQUID FROM ZUCCHINI AND STIR INTO TOMATO MIXTURE. SPRINKLE EACH TOMATO SHELL WITH A LITTLE BROWN SUGAR. PLACE SHELLS IN AN OVENPROOF DISH. SPOON ZUCCHINI MIXTURE INTO EACH. SPRINKLE WITH PARMESAN CHEESE. BAKE AT 350°F FOR 25 MINUTES. GARNISH TOPS WITH MINCED PARSLEY. SERVES 8.

— 6.3 GRAMS FAT PER SERVING

DILLED VEGETABLES

A NEW BUFFET OR FAMILY DINNER FAVORITE - SERVE AT ROOM TEMPERATURE.

3 LARGE HEADS BROCCOLI, CUT INTO FLORETS
1 LARGE CAULIFLOWER, CUT INTO FLORETS
3-4 CARROTS, CUT IN 1/4" ROUNDS

DRESSING

1/3 CUP OLIVE OIL	75 mL
2-3 TBSP. WHITE WINE VINEGAR	30-45 mL
1 TBSP. DIJON MUSTARD	15 mL
1 TBSP. SUGAR	15 mL
1 1/2 TSP. DRIED DILL	7 mL
3/4 TSP. SALT	4 mL
3/4 TSP. CURRY OR PAPRIKA	4 mL

IN A LARGE POT BRING 4 CUPS OF WATER TO A BOIL. ADD ALL VEGGIES AND COOK UNTIL TENDER-CRISP (2-3 MINUTES). DRAIN AND RINSE IMMEDIATELY UNDER COLD WATER. WHISK DRESSING INGREDIENTS TOGETHER. COVER AND SET ASIDE UNTIL SERVING TIME. POUR OVER VEGETABLES AND MIX GENTLY TO COAT. SERVES 14.

 5.8 GRAMS FAT PER SERVING

TOADS ARE FASTER THAN FROGS - YOU NEVER SEE TOADS' LEGS ON A MENU.

ORANGE SESAME CARROTS

1 LB. CARROTS (ABOUT 6)	500 g
1 TBSP. TOASTED SESAME SEEDS	15 mL
2 TBSP. ORANGE JUICE	30 mL
1 TSP. GRATED FRESH GINGER	5 mL
1 TSP. SESAME OIL	5 mL
1 TSP. SOY SAUCE	5 mL
SALT AND PEPPER TO TASTE	

PEEL CARROTS, CUT IN STICKS, AND STEAM ABOUT 8 MINUTES, UNTIL TENDER-CRISP. COMBINE TOASTED SESAME SEEDS, JUICE, GINGER, OIL AND SOY SAUCE. TOSS WITH CARROTS AND SEASON WITH SALT AND PEPPER. SERVES 4.

2.8 GRAMS FAT PER SERVING.

"WHAT'S YOUR SON WANT TO BE WHEN HE GRADUATES FROM COLLEGE?"

"I'M NOT SURE, BUT JUDGING FROM THE LETTERS HE WRITES HOME, I'D SAY HE WAS GOING TO BE A PROFESSIONAL FUNDRAISER."

LIGHTEN-UP SCALLOPED POTATOES!

THE NAME SAYS IT ALL!

1 TBSP. OLIVE OIL	15 mL
2 CUPS THINLY SLICED ONIONS	500 mL
1 BAY LEAF	
VEGETABLE SPRAY	
2 LBS. BAKING POTATOES, PEELED AND	1 Kg
THINLY SLICED	
NUTMEG TO TASTE	
SALT & PEPPER TO TASTE	
1½ CUPS CHICKEN BROTH	375 mL

HEAT OIL IN NONSTICK PAN OVER MEDIUM-LOW HEAT. ADD ONIONS AND BAY LEAF AND SAUTÉ UNTIL GOLDEN AND TENDER (ABOUT 10-15 MINUTES). DISCARD THE BAY LEAF. PREHEAT OVEN TO 425°F. SPRAY A DEEP-DISH PIE PLATE WITH VEGETABLE SPRAY. LAYER ⅓ OF THE ONIONS AND POTATOES EVENLY. SEASON WITH NUTMEG, SALT AND PEPPER. REPEAT LAYERS, OVERLAPPING POTATO SLICES, ENDING WITH THE SEASONING. POUR THE CHICKEN BROTH OVER TOP. BAKE FOR 30 MINUTES, REDUCE HEAT TO 350°F AND BAKE 20-25 MINUTES LONGER, UNTIL TOP IS GOLDEN BROWN AND POTATOES ARE TENDER. SERVES 4.

4.1 GRAMS FAT PER SERVING

IF YOU'RE GOING TO TRY CROSS-COUNTRY SKIING, START WITH A SMALL COUNTRY.

GRUYÈRE SCALLOPED POTATOES

2 GARLIC CLOVES, MINCED
2½ CUPS HALF & HALF CREAM   625 mL
6 BAKING POTATOES, PEELED
2 TBSP. FLOUR   30 mL
3 CUPS GRATED GRUYÈRE CHEESE   750 mL
SALT AND PEPPER TO TASTE

STIR GARLIC INTO CREAM AND SET ASIDE. SLICE POTATOES INTO PAPER-THIN ROUNDS AND TOSS WITH FLOUR. ARRANGE HALF THE POTATOES IN A 9" X 13" GLASS BAKING DISH. SPRINKLE WITH HALF OF THE CHEESE AND POUR HALF OF THE CREAM MIXTURE OVER TOP. SPRINKLE WITH SALT AND PEPPER. REPEAT LAYERS. COVER AND BAKE AT 325°F FOR 1 HOUR. REMOVE COVER AND CONTINUE BAKING FOR ½ HOUR, OR UNTIL POTATOES ARE TENDER.

MAN AT BAKERY: "INSIDE ME, THERE'S A THIN PERSON STRUGGLING TO GET OUT. BUT I CAN USUALLY SEDATE HIM WITH FOUR OR FIVE DOUGHNUTS."

COCONUT RICE

THE VERY THING FOR SPICY FOOD: GREEK LAMB STEW (PAGE 159) OR THIGH CHICKEN (PAGE 132).

2 CUPS BASMATI RICE, WASHED AND RINSED	500 mL
14-OZ. CAN COCONUT MILK	398 mL
2 1/4 CUPS WATER	550 mL
1 TSP. SALT	5 mL
1 TSP. SUGAR	5 mL
1 CINNAMON STICK	

IN LARGE SAUCEPAN WITH TIGHT-FITTING LID, MIX RICE WITH REMAINING INGREDIENTS. BRING TO A BOIL AND REDUCE HEAT TO LOW. COOK, COVERED, FOR 25 MINUTES, OR UNTIL LIQUID IS ABSORBED. REMOVE CINNAMON STICK. SERVES 8.

GADGET: ANY MECHANICAL DEVICE THAT PERFORMS A KITCHEN TASK IN ONE TWENTIETH OF THE TIME IT TAKES TO FIND IT.

BROWN AND WILD RICE CASSEROLE

CRUNCHY AND TASTY - GREAT FOR BARBECUES.

6 OZ.-PKG BROWN AND WILD RICE (OMIT SPICE PKG.)	170 g
1 TSP. SALT	5 mL
½ CUP COARSELY CHOPPED PECANS	125 mL
2 TBSP. CHOPPED GREEN ONION	30 mL
2 TBSP. BUTTER	30 mL
1½ CUPS SLICED MUSHROOMS	375 mL
ZEST OF 1 SMALL ORANGE	
ZEST OF 1 SMALL LEMON	
WHITE PEPPER	

PREPARE RICE ACCORDING TO PACKAGE DIRECTIONS, OMITTING THE SPICE PACKAGE AND ADDING THE SALT. SAUTÉ PECANS AND GREEN ONIONS IN BUTTER UNTIL TOASTED. STIR IN MUSHROOMS AND COOK 2 MINUTES. COMBINE PECAN MIXTURE WITH RICE. STIR IN ORANGE AND LEMON ZEST. SEASON TO TASTE WITH PEPPER. SERVES 4.

ENJOY YOUR KIDS WHILE THEY'RE STILL YOUNG AND ON YOUR SIDE.

KIWI SALSA

REFRESHING! SERVE WITH GRILLED CHICKEN OR FISH.

MARINADE

2 TBSP. LIME JUICE	30 mL
1 TBSP. OLIVE OIL	15 mL
1 JALAPENO PEPPER, SEEDED AND MINCED	
1 TSP. HONEY	5 mL
1 GARLIC CLOVE, MINCED	
1 TSP. CURRY	5 mL
1 TSP. CUMIN	5 mL
1/4 TSP. HOT RED PEPPER FLAKES	1 mL

6 KIWI FRUIT, PEELED AND DICED
1 SMALL ONION, PEELED AND DICED

MIX MARINADE INGREDIENTS IN SMALL BOWL. ADD KIWI AND ONION. STIR AND LET STAND AT ROOM TEMPERATURE FOR AT LEAST 1 HOUR. REFRIGERATE UNTIL READY TO SERVE. MAKES 2 CUPS.

LESS THAN 2 GRAMS FAT IN A 1/4 CUP SERVING

AN EXPERT IS SOMEONE WHO IS BROUGHT IN AT THE LAST MINUTE TO SHARE THE BLAME.

ROASTED ORANGE PEPPER AND CORN SALSA

GOOD ON TACOS AND FAJITAS.

3 YELLOW PEPPERS, HALVED AND SEEDED	
1/2 CUP CHICKEN BROTH	125 mL
1/2 TSP. CUMIN	2 mL
SALT AND PEPPER TO TASTE	
19-OZ. CAN KERNEL CORN	540 mL
1/4-1/2 TSP. HOT RED PEPPER FLAKES	1-2 mL

PLACE PEPPER HALVES CUT-SIDE DOWN ON A COOKIE SHEET. BROIL UNTIL SKINS ARE BLACKENED AND PUFFED. LEAVE SKINS ON AND PLACE IN SAUCEPAN, ADD CHICKEN BROTH AND COOK UNCOVERED 10 MINUTES. PURÉE WITH CUMIN, SALT AND PEPPER. ADD CORN AND PEPPER FLAKES. STORE IN REFRIGERATOR. MAKES 2 CUPS. (PICTURED ON PAGE 17.)

3.7 GRAMS FAT IN 2 CUPS

IT ISN'T EASY BEING THE PARENT OF A SIX-YEAR-OLD. ON THE OTHER HAND, IT'S A SMALL PRICE TO PAY TO HAVE SOMEONE AROUND WHO UNDERSTANDS COMPUTERS.

GREAT FOR BARBECUES. ALSO DELICIOUS ON RIBS IF YOU'RE NOT COUNTING FAT.

½ CUP DIJON MUSTARD	125 mL
¼ CUP TARRAGON WINE VINEGAR	60 mL
2 TBSP. BROWN SUGAR	30 mL
1 TBSP. DRY MUSTARD	15 mL
¼ CUP HONEY	60 mL

COMBINE ALL INGREDIENTS.

FOR BARBECUED CHICKEN: YOU NEED ENOUGH SKINLESS CHICKEN PIECES FOR THE CROWD. BARBECUE CHICKEN OVER MEDIUM HEAT UNTIL NO LONGER PINK IN MIDDLE. BRUSH WITH SAUCE AND CONTINUE COOKING, TURNING FREQUENTLY UNTIL MEAT IS DONE.

 5.5 GRAMS FAT IN 1 CUP SAUCE

YOU KNOW YOU'RE IN TROUBLE WHEN YOU GO TO PUT ON THE CLOTHES YOU WORE HOME FROM THE PARTY.....AND THERE AREN'T ANY.

⅓ CUP OIL	75 mL
1 MEDIUM ONION, CHOPPED	
¼ CUP PARSLEY, CHOPPED	60 mL
2 GARLIC CLOVES, MINCED	
1 CUP VINEGAR	250 mL
¾ CUP BROWN SUGAR	175 mL
7½-OZ. CAN TOMATO SAUCE	213 mL
⅔ CUP WORCESTERSHIRE SAUCE	150 mL
¼ TSP. TABASCO SAUCE	1 mL
1 TSP. ROSEMARY	5 mL
½ TSP. THYME	2 mL
2 TSP. SALT	10 mL

HEAT OIL AND SAUTÉ ONION AND PARSLEY. ADD REMAINING INGREDIENTS AND SIMMER UNTIL THICKENED (ABOUT AN HOUR - THE LONGER THE BETTER!). STORE IN A JAR IN REFRIGERATOR AND USE AS A SAUCE FOR BEEF OR PORK.

ECONOMISTS REPORT THAT A COLLEGE EDUCATION ADDS MANY THOUSANDS OF DOLLARS TO A PERSON'S LIFETIME INCOME - WHICH THEY SPEND SENDING THEIR CHILDREN TO COLLEGE.

FAST AND EASY PIZZA CRUST

PUT THIS TOGETHER WHEN YOU COME HOME FROM WORK - TAKES ABOUT 20 MINUTES.

½ CUP WARM WATER	125 mL
1 PKG. ACTIVE DRY YEAST (1 TBSP.)	15 mL
1 TSP. SUGAR	5 mL
1 ½ CUPS FLOUR	375 mL
¼ TSP. SALT	1 mL
1 TBSP. YELLOW CORNMEAL	15 mL
1 TBSP. OLIVE OIL	15 mL
CORNMEAL TO SPRINKLE	

PREHEAT OVEN TO 450°F. LIGHTLY OIL A 12" PIZZA PAN. IN A SMALL BOWL, MIX WARM WATER, YEAST AND SUGAR TOGETHER. LET SIT UNTIL YEAST ACTIVATES (ABOUT 5 MINUTES). IN A LARGE BOWL, STIR TOGETHER FLOUR, SALT AND CORNMEAL. ADD YEAST MIXTURE AND OLIVE OIL AND KNEAD TO A SMOOTH DOUGH (ABOUT 10 MINUTES). SPRINKLE A WORK SURFACE WITH CORNMEAL AND ROLL DOUGH INTO A 13" CIRCLE. LINE PIZZA PAN WITH DOUGH. CRIMP EDGES AND ADD YOUR FAVORITE TOPPINGS. BAKE FOR 10-15 MINUTES. MAKES 1, 12" PIZZA.

SOME RELATIVES ARE LIKE FIRES - THE SOONER THEY'RE OUT, THE BETTER.

PEAR AND CAMBOZOLA PIZZA

THIS IS SOOO GOOD!

12" PIZZA CRUST (PAGE 96) OR PURCHASED	30 cm
OLIVE OIL TO BRUSH ON CRUST	
14-OZ. CAN PEARS, DRAINED AND SLICED	398 mL
IN THIN STRIPS	
2 TBSP. TOASTED PINE NUTS	30 mL
3 OZ. CAMBOZOLA CHEESE, SLICED	85 g
FRESHLY GROUND PEPPER	

PREHEAT OVEN TO 450°F. BRUSH CRUST WITH OLIVE OIL, ARRANGE PEARS ON CRUST IN PINWHEEL PATTERN, SPRINKLE WITH PINE NUTS, TOP WITH CHEESE AND A SPRINKLE OF PEPPER. BAKE 10-15 MINUTES UNTIL CRUST IS GOLDEN. (PICTURED ON PAGE 105.)

ANOTHER GOOD IDEA: FOR APPLE AND BRIE PIZZA, SAUTÉ SLICED APPLES IN BUTTER AND BROWN SUGAR. SPRINKLE WITH CINNAMON. DOT CRUST WITH BROKEN PIECES OF BRIE CHEESE, ARRANGE APPLES ON TOP AND SPRINKLE WITH CHOPPED WALNUTS AND FRESH ROSEMARY. BAKE AS ABOVE.

SHE'S DESCENDED FROM A LONG LINE HER MOTHER LISTENED TO.

PESTO PIZZA

12" PIZZA CRUST (PAGE 96) OR PURCHASED   30 cm
6½-oz. JAR MARINATED ARTICHOKES,   184 mL
    RESERVE MARINADE
3 OZ. CAMBOZOLA CHEESE, SLICED   85 g
BASIL PESTO SAUCE (PAGE 69)
FRESH BASIL LEAVES
MARINATED SUN-DRIED TOMATOES (PAGE 101)
FRESH ROMA TOMATOES, SLICED
FRESHLY GROUND PEPPER

PREHEAT OVEN TO 450°F. PREPARE PIZZA CRUST. DRAIN ARTICHOKE HEARTS AND BRUSH CRUST WITH SOME OF RESERVED MARINADE. PLACE CHEESE ON CRUST LEAVING ½" BORDER AND SPREAD WITH PESTO SAUCE. TOP WITH REMAINING INGREDIENTS (DON'T FORGET THE DRAINED ARTICHOKES!). BAKE 10-15 MINUTES, UNTIL CRUST IS GOLDEN. REMOVE FROM OVEN - IT'S READY - IT'S DELICIOUS!

THE BEST TIME TO PUT CHILDREN TO BED IS WHENEVER THEY'LL GO.

CARAMELIZED ONION AND CHÈVRE PIZZA

PIZZA IMPROMPTU AND MIGHTY TASTY TOO!

12" PIZZA CRUST (PAGE 96) OR PURCHASED	30 cm
OLIVE OIL TO BRUSH CRUST	
3 MEDIUM ONIONS, THINLY SLICED (USE ALL 3!)	
1 TBSP. BUTTER	15 mL
2 TBSP. OLIVE OIL	30 mL
1 TBSP. SUGAR	15 mL
3 TBSP. BALSAMIC VINEGAR	45 mL
SALT TO TASTE	
2 CUPS GRATED OR CRUMBLED CHÈVRE (GOAT'S CHEESE)	500 mL
½ CUP TOASTED PINE NUTS	125 mL
FRESHLY GROUND PEPPER	

PREHEAT OVEN TO 450°F. BRUSH CRUST WITH OLIVE OIL. IN A LARGE FRYING PAN OVER LOW HEAT, COMBINE ONIONS, BUTTER AND OLIVE OIL. COVER AND COOK, STIRRING OFTEN, UNTIL ONIONS ARE VERY SOFT, ABOUT 30 MINUTES. ADD SUGAR AND VINEGAR AND CONTINUE COOKING UNTIL VINEGAR EVAPORATES, ABOUT 5 MINUTES. ADD SALT TO TASTE. PLACE CHEESE ON CRUST LEAVING ½" BORDER. SPRINKLE WITH PINE NUTS, TOP WITH ONION MIXTURE AND A SPRINKLE OF FRESHLY GROUND PEPPER. BAKE 10-15 MINUTES UNTIL CRUST IS GOLDEN.

WHAT'S THE DIFFERENCE BETWEEN AN ONION AND AN ACCORDIAN? NO ONE CRIES WHEN YOU CHOP UP AN ACCORDIAN.

12" PIZZA CRUST (PAGE 96) OR PURCHASED

30 cm

GRATED MOZZARELLA CHEESE

TOPPINGS

MARINATED ARTICHOKE HEARTS, RESERVE MARINADE

ASPARAGUS TIPS OR BROCCOLI FLORETS

RED PEPPER CUT IN THIN STRIPS

MARINATED SUN-DRIED TOMATOES, CUT IN THIN SLIVERS (PAGE 101)

ROMA TOMATOES, THINLY SLICED

FETA CHEESE, CRUMBLED

BASIL, DRIED OR FRESH

PITTED OLIVES, SLICED

GRATED MOZZARELLA CHEESE TO SPRINKLE

PREHEAT OVEN TO 450°F. BRUSH CRUST WITH SOME OF RESERVED ARTICHOKE MARINADE. SPRINKLE WITH ANY OR ALL OF THE TOPPINGS LISTED. TOP WITH MORE CHEESE AND BAKE 10-15 MINUTES, OR UNTIL CRUST IS GOLDEN. (PICTURED ON PAGE 105.)

YOU KNOW YOU'RE IN TROUBLE WHEN YOU CALL YOUR WIFE AND TELL HER YOU'D LIKE TO EAT OUT TONIGHT - AND WHEN YOU GET HOME, THERE'S A SANDWICH ON THE FRONT PORCH.

MARINATED SUN-DRIED TOMATOES

LESS EXPENSIVE THAN STORE-BOUGHT!

3-OZ. PKG. SUN-DRIED TOMATOES	85 g
BOILING WATER TO COVER	
½ CUP OLIVE OIL	125 mL
3 GARLIC CLOVES, MINCED	
2 TBSP. FRESH CHOPPED OREGANO OR	30 mL
1 TSP. (5 mL) DRIED	
2 TBSP. FRESH CHOPPED BASIL OR	30 mL
1 TSP. (5 mL) DRIED	

PLACE SUN-DRIED TOMATOES IN SMALL BOWL. COVER WITH BOILING WATER AND SOAK 2-3 MINUTES. DRAIN, SLICE AND RETURN TO BOWL. ADD OIL AND REMAINING INGREDIENTS. LET STAND AT LEAST 1 HOUR, STIRRING OCCASIONALLY. STORE IN REFRIGERATOR. OLIVE OIL WILL CONGEAL - WARM IN MICROWAVE OR HOT WATER BEFORE USING.

RECENT COLLEGE GRADUATE: "I WAS ON THE DEAN'S LIST, BUT NOBODY IN THE EMPLOYMENT OFFICES SEEMS TO KNOW THE DEAN!"

RANCHERO SAUCE

2 TBSP. VEGETABLE OIL	30 mL
1 CUP FINELY CHOPPED ONION	250 mL
1 GARLIC CLOVE, MINCED	
4 CUPS FINELY CHOPPED FRESH OR CANNED TOMATOES	1 L
2 ANAHEIM OR OTHER MILD CHILIES, CORED, SEEDED AND CHOPPED	
1 TSP. SUGAR	5 mL
SALT AND FRESHLY GROUND PEPPER TO TASTE	
2 TBSP. MINCED CILANTRO	30 mL
12" PIZZA CRUST (PAGE 96) OR PURCHASED	30 cm

TOPPING

1 CUP RANCHERO SAUCE	250 mL
1/2 LB. HOT SAUSAGE, COOKED, CRUMBLED AND DRAINED	250 g
1 1/2 CUPS GRATED MONTEREY JACK CHEESE	375 mL
1/2 CUP THINLY SLICED RED ONION	125 mL
1 RED, YELLOW OR GREEN BELL PEPPER, SLICED IN STRIPS	
1 PICKLED JALAPEÑO CHILI, SEEDED AND DICED	

TO PREPARE SAUCE: IN LARGE SKILLET, HEAT OIL OVER MEDIUM HEAT AND ADD ONION. COOK 2 MINUTES, STIRRING CONSTANTLY. ADD GARLIC AND COOK 2 MINUTES MORE, OR UNTIL ONION IS TRANSLUCENT. ADD TOMATOES, CHILIES, SUGAR, SALT AND PEPPER. SIMMER UNTIL SLIGHTLY THICKENED (ABOUT 15 MINUTES), STIRRING OCCASIONALLY. STIR IN CILANTRO.

MEXICAN PIZZA

THIS RECIPE CONTINUED FROM PAGE 102.

THIS RECIPE MAKES 4 CUPS AND WILL KEEP REFRIGERATED FOR UP TO 1 WEEK. ALSO DELICIOUS USED AS A PASTA SAUCE.

TO PREPARE PIZZA: PREHEAT OVEN TO 500°F. SPREAD RANCHERO SAUCE EVENLY OVER PIZZA DOUGH. COVER WITH COOKED SAUSAGE AND SPRINKLE CHEESE OVER ALL. EVENLY DISTRIBUTE ONION, PEPPER AND PICKLED JALAPEÑO OVER CHEESE. BAKE PIZZA IN THE LOWER THIRD OF OVEN UNTIL CRUST IS BROWNED AND CHEESE IS MELTED - ABOUT 15-20 MINUTES. (PICTURED ON PAGE 105.)

BEFORE MARRIAGE, A MAN WILL LIE AWAKE ALL NIGHT THINKING ABOUT SOMETHING YOU SAID; AFTER MARRIAGE, HE'LL FALL ASLEEP BEFORE YOU FINISH SAYING IT.

ORIENTAL CHICKEN PIZZA

THAT'LL BE YOUR ORIENTAL ITALIAN DINNER!

1 WHOLE CHICKEN BREAST, SKINNED, BONED AND HALVED	
2 TBSP. TERIYAKI SAUCE	30 mL
12" PIZZA CRUST, (PAGE 96) OR PURCHASED	30 cm
SESAME OIL TO BRUSH ON CRUST	
2 TBSP. GRATED FRESH GINGER	30 mL
1 GARLIC CLOVE, MINCED	
3/4 CUP GRATED ASIAGO CHEESE	175 mL
3/4 CUP GRATED MOZZARELLA CHEESE	175 mL
1 HANDFUL PEA PODS, CUT IN THIN STRIPS	
OR 1/2 GREEN PEPPER, CUT IN THIN STRIPS	
1/2 RED PEPPER, CUT IN STRIPS	
2-3 GREEN ONIONS, CUT IN STRIPS	
HOT RED PEPPER FLAKES TO SPRINKLE	

BRUSH CHICKEN WITH TERIYAKI SAUCE. GRILL CHICKEN 3 MINUTES PER SIDE AND SLICE IN STRIPS. PREHEAT OVEN TO 450°F. BRUSH CRUST WITH SESAME OIL, SPRINKLE WITH GINGER, GARLIC AND CHEESES. TOP WITH CHICKEN AND VEGGIES. SPRINKLE WITH HOT PEPPER FLAKES AND BAKE 15 MINUTES, OR UNTIL CRUST IS GOLDEN.

ASK YOUR CHILD WHAT HE WANTS FOR DINNER ONLY IF HE'S BUYING.

PICTURED ON OVERLEAF

PEAR AND CAMBOZOLA PIZZA
    - PAGE 97
PIZZA PRIMAVERA - PAGE 100
MEXICAN PIZZA - PAGE 102

LEMON FETTUCCINE

DEE-LICIOUS AND INCREDIBLY EASY. SERVE WITH GRILLED SHRIMP OR CHICKEN.

¾ LB. FETTUCCINE	365 g
¼ CUP MELTED BUTTER	60 mL
1 CUP WHIPPING CREAM	250 mL
1 LEMON, JUICE AND GRATED RIND	
½ CUP PINE NUTS	125 mL

COOK PASTA ACCORDING TO PACKAGE DIRECTIONS. COMBINE BUTTER, WHIPPING CREAM, LEMON JUICE AND GRATED RIND. TOSS WITH PASTA AND PINE NUTS. SERVES 4.

CALORIES ARE LITTLE UNITS THAT MEASURE HOW GOOD A PARTICULAR FOOD TASTES. FUDGE, FOR EXAMPLE, HAS A GREAT MANY CALORIES, WHEREAS CELERY, WHICH IS NOT REALLY A FOOD BUT A MEMBER OF THE PLYWOOD FAMILY PROVIDED BY MOTHER NATURE SO THAT WE WOULD HAVE A WAY TO GET ONION DIP INTO OUR MOUTHS, HAS NONE.   - DAVE BARRY

GORGONZOLA PASTA

RICH CREAMY BLUE CHEESE SAUCE. MAMA MIA!

1 CUP WHIPPING CREAM	250 mL
1/2 LB. GORGONZOLA CHEESE	250 g
(STILTON IS A GOOD SUBSTITUTE)	
2 TBSP. BUTTER	30 mL
1/4 TSP. NUTMEG	1 mL
1/3 CUP FRESHLY GRATED	75 mL
PARMESAN CHEESE	
1 LB. SPAGHETTI OR LINGUINE	500 g
GRATED PARMESAN CHEESE TO SPRINKLE	
FRESHLY GROUND PEPPER	
CHOPPED FRESH PARSLEY FOR GARNISH	

IN HEAVY SAUCEPAN, COOK CREAM UNTIL IT BOILS
AND IS SLIGHTLY THICKENED. LOWER HEAT, ADD
CRUMBLED CHEESE, BUTTER AND NUTMEG. STIR
UNTIL ALL INGREDIENTS HAVE MELTED AND
SAUCE IS WELL-BLENDED. STIR IN PARMESAN.
COOK PASTA AS DIRECTED. DRAIN AND COMBINE
HOT PASTA WITH SAUCE. SERVE WITH EXTRA
PARMESAN AND GROUND PEPPER. SPRINKLE WITH
CHOPPED PARSLEY. YOU DIDN'T LOSE ANY WEIGHT,
BUT YOU SURE MADE A LOT OF FRIENDS! SERVE
WITH MIXED GREENS AND ITALIAN DRESSING
(PAGE 67).

ABSTINENCE MAKES THE HEART GROW FONDER.

ACCEPTABLE FETTUCCINE ALFREDO

YOU JUST EARNED YOUR HALO!

¾ LB. FETTUCCINE	365 g
1 CUP 1% COTTAGE CHEESE	250 mL
¼ CUP PARMESAN CHEESE	60 mL
¼ CUP SKIM MILK	60 mL
1 EGG	
1 TSP. POWDERED CHICKEN BOUILLON	5 mL
¼ TSP. NUTMEG	1 mL
SALT & PEPPER TO TASTE	
½ CUP CHOPPED FRESH BASIL OR PARSLEY	125 mL

COOK PASTA ACCORDING TO PACKAGE DIRECTIONS,
DRAIN AND RETURN TO SAUCEPAN. PROCESS
COTTAGE CHEESE UNTIL SMOOTH. ADD REMAINING
INGREDIENTS AND PROCESS UNTIL BLENDED.
POUR SAUCE OVER WARM PASTA, FOLD IN GENTLY
AND SERVE. SERVES 4.

5 GRAMS FAT PER SERVING

NOWADAYS, WHEN YOU GET RIGHT DOWN TO BRASS
TACKS, THEY'RE PLASTIC.

TORTELLINI WITH THREE CHEESES

A NIFTY NEW PASTA CASSEROLE FOR YOUR FAMILY.

12-OZ. PKG. VEAL TORTELLINI	350 g
3 TBSP. MARGARINE	45 mL
1 CUP FRESH BREAD CRUMBS	250 mL
1 TSP. DRIED BASIL	5 mL
OR 1 TBSP (15 mL) FRESH	
2 GARLIC CLOVES, MINCED	
1 SMALL ONION, CHOPPED	
4 TSP. FLOUR	20 mL
2 CUPS SKIM MILK	500 mL
1 TSP. DRIED BASIL	5 mL
OR 1 TBSP. (15 mL) FRESH	
SALT AND PEPPER TO TASTE	
1 CUP GRATED SKIM MILK	250 mL
MOZZARELLA CHEESE	
1 CUP RICOTTA CHEESE	250 mL
½ CUP FRESHLY GRATED	125 mL
PARMESAN CHEESE	
1½ CUPS FROZEN PEAS	375 mL

COOK TORTELLINI ACCORDING TO PACKAGE
DIRECTIONS. DRAIN AND TRANSFER TO LARGE
CASSEROLE. IN A LARGE SKILLET, MELT
MARGARINE. TRANSFER 1 TBSP. TO SMALL BOWL,
STIR IN BREAD CRUMBS AND BASIL. SET ASIDE.
ADD GARLIC AND ONION TO SKILLET. COOK OVER
MEDIUM HEAT UNTIL ONION IS SOFTENED. SPRINKLE
WITH FLOUR AND STIR FOR 1 MINUTE. GRADUALLY
STIR IN MILK. SPRINKLE WITH BASIL, SALT AND
PEPPER. COOK 2-3 MINUTES UNTIL THICKENED.
STIR IN MOZZARELLA, RICOTTA AND PARMESAN
CHEESES. POUR OVER TORTELLINI. RINSE PEAS
UNDER HOT WATER AND GENTLY STIR INTO
CASSEROLE. SPRINKLE WITH BREAD CRUMBS AND
BAKE, UNCOVERED, AT 375°F FOR 30 MINUTES.
SERVES 6. PERFECT WITH DILL AND PARMESAN
TOMATOES ("GRAND SLAM" - PAGE 99).

FRESH TOMATO & CHEESE PASTA

BOW TIE PASTA FOR 4
2 GARLIC CLOVES, MINCED
2 CUPS QUARTERED, FRESH ROMA   500 mL
    TOMATOES (6)
2 TBSP. OLIVE OIL   30 mL
½ CUP FRESH BASIL, CHOPPED   125 mL
½ LB. BRIE CHEESE, REMOVE RIND   250 g
½ CUP PINE NUTS, TOASTED (OPTIONAL)   125 mL
FRESHLY GROUND SALT AND PEPPER TO TASTE
CHOPPED PARSLEY
PARMESAN CHEESE

COOK PASTA ACCORDING TO PACKAGE DIRECTIONS.
SAUTÉ GARLIC AND TOMATOES IN OLIVE OIL. ADD
BASIL AND PINCHED-OFF PIECES OF BRIE
CHEESE. STIR UNTIL CHEESE IS PARTIALLY
MELTED. ADD PINE NUTS. SPRINKLE WITH SALT
AND PEPPER. ADD COOKED PASTA TO PAN AND
GENTLY MIX ALL INGREDIENTS. PLACE IN PASTA
BOWL AND SPRINKLE WITH PARSLEY AND
PARMESAN CHEESE. SERVE WITH A GREEN SALAD
AND GARLIC TOAST.

PEOPLE WHO KNOW HOW TO LAUGH AT THEMSELVES
WILL NEVER CEASE TO BE AMUSED.

TART AND TASTY - SERVE HOT AS MAIN DISH OR COLD AS A PASTA SALAD.

DRESSING

2 TBSP. FRESH CHOPPED BASIL OR	30 mL
1 TBSP. (15 mL) DRIED	
1/3 CUP LEMON JUICE	75 mL
2 GARLIC CLOVES, MINCED	
2 TBSP. CAPERS	30 mL
1/2 TSP. NUTMEG	2 mL
1 TBSP. BALSAMIC VINEGAR	15 mL
OIL FROM MARINATED ARTICHOKES	

PASTA

2 CUPS UNCOOKED ROTINI OR FUSILLI	500 mL
1 EACH RED, ORANGE AND GREEN PEPPER,	
SLICED IN STRIPS	
1 MEDIUM RED ONION, THINLY SLICED	
3 CARROTS, SLICED DIAGONALLY	
2 GARLIC CLOVES, MINCED	
2 TBSP. OLIVE OIL	30 mL
2 - 6-OZ. JARS MARINATED ARTICHOKES,	2 - 170 g
DRAINED, RESERVE OIL	

TO PREPARE DRESSING: IN A BLENDER, COMBINE ALL DRESSING INGREDIENTS.

TO PREPARE PASTA: COOK ACCORDING TO PACKAGE DIRECTIONS. MEANWHILE, STIR-FRY VEGGIES AND GARLIC IN OIL. ADD DRAINED MARINATED ARTICHOKES AND FOLD INTO COOKED PASTA. PLACE IN A HEATED BOWL AND TOSS WITH DESIRED AMOUNT OF DRESSING (STORE EXTRA IN REFRIGERATOR). SERVES 6.

PASTA WITH SPINACH AND FETA CHEESE

PASTA PERFECTA!

6 TBSP. OLIVE OIL	90 mL
3 MEDIUM RED ONIONS (YOU DO NEED ALL OF THEM), FINELY SLICED	
2 GARLIC CLOVES, MINCED	
1 BUNCH FRESH SPINACH (ADD MORE, IF YOU'RE INTO IRON!)	
SALT TO SPRINKLE	
3 CUPS UNCOOKED FUSILLI (TRY THE COLORED FOR A CHANGE)	750 mL
1 CUP CRUMBLED FETA CHEESE	250 mL
FRESHLY GRATED PARMESAN CHEESE	
PEPPER, FRESHLY GRATED	
1/4 CUP TOASTED PINE NUTS (OPTIONAL)	60 mL
1/4 CUP SLICED KALAMATA OLIVES (OPTIONAL)	60 mL

HEAT OIL IN SAUCEPAN. ADD ONIONS AND GARLIC AND SAUTÉ FOR 10 MINUTES. ADD SPINACH AND SPRINKLE LIGHTLY WITH SALT. STIR UNTIL SPINACH WILTS. COVER AND COOK OVER LOW HEAT FOR 10 MINUTES. COOK PASTA UNTIL TENDER. DRAIN. ADD FETA CHEESE TO WARM PASTA AND COOK OVER LOW HEAT UNTIL CHEESE MELTS. ADD SPINACH MIXTURE AND TOSS. SPRINKLE WITH PARMESAN CHEESE, PEPPER, PINE NUTS AND OLIVES IF DESIRED.

SIGN ON COMMUNITY BULLETIN BOARD: FREE KITTENS - AGAIN!!

A HEALTHY PASTA-BILITY - NOW THAT'S USING YOUR NOODLE!

1 TBSP. MARGARINE	15 mL
1 ONION, CHOPPED	
2 GARLIC CLOVES, MINCED	
2 CUPS SLICED MUSHROOMS	500 mL
1 RED PEPPER CUT IN THIN STRIPS	
1 BUNCH FRESH ASPARAGUS, SLICED	
2 CARROTS, CHOPPED	
1 LARGE ZUCCHINI, CHOPPED	
1/2 CUP CHOPPED FRESH BASIL, DIVIDED	125 mL
SALT AND PEPPER TO TASTE	
2 TBSP. FLOUR	30 mL
13½-OZ. CAN EVAPORATED SKIM MILK	385 mL
2 CUPS FUSILLI PASTA	500 mL
1/4 CUP FRESHLY GRATED PARMESAN CHEESE	

IN SKILLET, MELT MARGARINE AND COOK THE ONION, GARLIC AND MUSHROOMS ABOUT 5 MINUTES. ADD REMAINING VEGGIES AND 2 TBSP. BASIL, SALT AND PEPPER. COVER AND COOK OVER MEDIUM HEAT FOR 5 MINUTES; UNCOVER AND COOK UNTIL ALL LIQUID HAS EVAPORATED. STIR IN FLOUR AND COOK STIRRING FOR 1 MINUTE. ADD MILK AND COOK STIRRING FOR 5 MINUTES UNTIL THICKENED. COOK PASTA ACCORDING TO PACKAGE DIRECTIONS. DRAIN AND TOSS WITH SAUCE. SPRINKLE WITH REMAINING BASIL AND PARMESAN CHEESE; TOSS AGAIN. SERVES 5.

7.9 GRAMS OF FAT PER SERVING

FETTUCCINE WITH SAMBUCA AND CRANBERRIES

PASTA FOR COMPANY - ¡ESTUPENDO!

2 WHOLE BONELESS CHICKEN BREASTS, SKINNED & CUBED	
1/4 CUP BUTTER	60 mL
2 GARLIC CLOVES, MINCED	
3 CUPS WHIPPING CREAM	750 mL
1/4 CUP SAMBUCA LIQUEUR	60 mL
1/4 CUP ORANGE JUICE CONCENTRATE	60 mL
1/2 CUP FRESHLY GRATED PARMESAN CHEESE	125 mL
1/4 TSP. NUTMEG	1 mL
SALT AND PEPPER TO TASTE	
14-OZ. CAN ARTICHOKES (10-12 COUNT), DRAINED AND CHOPPED	398 mL
3-OZ. PKG. DRIED CRANBERRIES	85 g
1 LB. FETTUCCINE	500 g

GARNISH

FRESH PARSLEY AND ORANGE ZEST

IN A LARGE FRYING PAN, HEAT BUTTER AND SAUTÉ CUBED CHICKEN AND GARLIC UNTIL BARELY COOKED (DO NOT OVER COOK!). REMOVE CHICKEN FROM PAN AND SET ASIDE. ADD WHIPPING CREAM, SAMBUCA AND ORANGE JUICE TO PAN AND STIR WELL. ADD PARMESAN, NUTMEG, SALT AND PEPPER, STIRRING UNTIL SMOOTH. SIMMER FOR 5 MINUTES. ADD CHOPPED ARTICHOKES, CRANBERRIES AND CHICKEN; SIMMER AND STIR FOR 10 MINUTES. THAT'S IT FOR THE SAUCE! NOW, COOK THE FETTUCCINE ACCORDING TO PACKAGE DIRECTIONS. CAREFULLY FOLD SAUCE INTO PASTA AND GARNISH WITH PARSLEY AND ORANGE ZEST. SERVE WITH GARLIC TOAST. SERVES 6-8.

THE WORKING GIRL'S PASTA.

1 LARGE WHITE ONION, CHOPPED	
2-4 GARLIC CLOVES, MINCED	
1 TBSP. OLIVE OIL	15 mL
2-3 ANCHOVIES	
28-OZ. CAN ITALIAN PLUM TOMATOES	796 mL
6-8 ROMA TOMATOES, PEELED AND CHOPPED	
1 CUP PITTED BLACK OLIVES, CHOPPED	250 mL
1/4 CUP LARGE CAPERS	60 mL
2 TBSP. BALSAMIC VINEGAR	30 mL
1/2 CUP CHOPPED FRESH BASIL	125 mL
HOT RED PEPPER FLAKES TO TASTE	
1/2 CUP RED WINE	125 mL
1/2 CUP CHOPPED FRESH CILANTRO	125 mL
FRESHLY GRATED PARMESAN CHEESE	
TAGLIATELLE, LINGUINE OR SPAGHETTI FOR 6	

SAUTÉ ONIONS AND GARLIC IN OIL. RINSE AND DRY ANCHOVIES AND CRUSH WITH A FORK INTO ONION-GARLIC MIXTURE. ADD ALL THE TOMATOES, OLIVES, CAPERS, BALSAMIC VINEGAR, BASIL, RED PEPPER FLAKES AND WINE. COOK ABOUT 1/2 HOUR STIRRING OCCASIONALLY UNTIL REDUCED AND THICKENED. SERVE OVER PASTA. GARNISH WITH CILANTRO AND PARMESAN. SERVES 6.

 12.0 GRAMS OF FAT PER SERVING

FLYING IS THE SECOND GREATEST THRILL KNOWN TO MAN. LANDING IS FIRST.

FETTUCCINE WITH ASPARAGUS AND SHRIMP

1 LB. LARGE SHRIMP, SHELLED AND DEVEINED	500 g
1 LEMON, JUICE AND GRATED RIND	
1/4-1/2 TSP. HOT RED PEPPER FLAKES	1-2 mL
1/2 TSP. SALT	2 mL
16-OZ. PKG. FETTUCCINE OR LINGUINE	500 g
1 TBSP. VEGETABLE OIL	15 mL
1 MEDIUM ONION, DICED	
2 RED PEPPERS, SLICED IN STRIPS	
1/2 TSP. SALT	2 mL
1 TBSP. VEGETABLE OIL	15 mL
1 LB. ASPARAGUS, CUT IN 3" PIECES	500 g
1/2 CUP WATER	125 mL
1 TBSP. SOY SAUCE	15 mL

IN A BOWL, MIX SHRIMP WITH LEMON JUICE, PEPPER FLAKES AND SALT. COOK FETTUCCINE ACCORDING TO PACKAGE DIRECTIONS. KEEP WARM IN POT. HEAT OIL AND STIR-FRY ONION, PEPPER STRIPS AND SALT UNTIL PEPPERS ARE TENDER-CRISP; REMOVE TO BOWL. IN SAME SKILLET HEAT OIL AND ADD ASPARAGUS AND SHRIMP MIXTURE. STIR-FRY UNTIL ASPARAGUS ARE TENDER-CRISP AND SHRIMP TURN OPAQUE (ABOUT 3 MINUTES). STIR IN PEPPER MIXTURE AND WATER; HEAT THROUGH. TO SERVE, TOSS FETTUCCINE WITH SHRIMP MIXTURE AND SOY SAUCE. SPRINKLE WITH GRATED LEMON RIND. SERVES 4. (PICTURED ON PAGE 123.)

11.2 GRAMS OF FAT PER SERVING

PASTA WITH SHRIMP AND FRESH TOMATO

2 TBSP. BUTTER	30 mL
1 ONION, CHOPPED	
4 GARLIC CLOVES, MINCED	
¼ CUP CHOPPED, FRESH PARSLEY	60 mL
1 LB. MEDIUM SHRIMP, UNCOOKED	500 mL
4 MEDIUM TOMATOES, CHOPPED	
½ CUP DRY WHITE WINE	125 mL
¼ TSP. HOT RED PEPPER FLAKES	1 mL
(OPTIONAL)	
SALT, PEPPER TO TASTE	
¾ LB. SPAGHETTI	365 mL

IN LARGE PAN, MELT BUTTER AND SAUTE ONION AND GARLIC. ADD PARSLEY AND SHRIMP; COOK 2 MINUTES. ADD TOMATOES, WINE AND SEASONINGS AND BRING TO A BOIL. COOK UNTIL SHRIMP TURN OPAQUE. DON'T OVERCOOK AS SHRIMP BECOME TOUGH. SET ASIDE. COOK PASTA AS DIRECTED. DRAIN. REHEAT SHRIMP MIXTURE AND SERVE IMMEDIATELY OVER PASTA. SERVES 4.

10 GRAMS OF FAT PER SERVING

HOW A BACHELOR SEPARATES HIS LAUNDRY: THESE ARE THE DIRTY CLOTHES THAT NEED WASHING - AND THESE ARE THE DIRTY CLOTHES THAT DON'T NEED WASHING.

VEGETABLE LASAGNE

1 MEDIUM ONION, CHOPPED	
8" ZUCCHINI, GRATED	20 cm
1 LARGE CARROT, GRATED	
4 CUPS SLICED FRESH MUSHROOMS	1 L
2 TBSP. OLIVE OIL	30 mL
½ TSP. THYME	2 mL
½ TSP. OREGANO	2 mL
½ TSP. BASIL	2 mL
3 CUPS SPAGHETTI SAUCE (HOT AND SPICY IS GOOD)	750 mL
9 LASAGNE NOODLES (OR USE OVEN-READY LASAGNE NOODLES)	
2 CUPS RICOTTA CHEESE	500 mL
3-4 CUPS FRESH SPINACH, CHOPPED	750 mL-1 L
3 CUPS GRATED MOZZARELLA CHEESE	750 mL

SAUTÉ ONION, ZUCCHINI, CARROT AND MUSHROOMS IN OIL UNTIL TENDER. ADD THYME, OREGANO AND BASIL. ADD SPAGHETTI SAUCE AND STIR TO COMBINE. SIMMER FOR 20 MINUTES. COOK LASAGNE NOODLES ACCORDING TO PACKAGE DIRECTIONS. GREASE A 9" X 13" CASSEROLE. LAYER WITH ½ OF THE SAUCE, 3 NOODLES, ½ OF THE RICOTTA CHEESE, COVER WITH ALL OF THE SPINACH, THEN ⅓ OF THE MOZZARELLA CHEESE. REPEAT LAYERS, ENDING WITH THE LAST 3 NOODLES AND MOZZARELLA. BAKE AT 350°F FOR 40 MINUTES, OR UNTIL BUBBLY. LET SIT FOR 5 MINUTES BEFORE CUTTING. SERVES 8.

MY WIFE SAYS I NEVER LISTEN TO HER... AT LEAST I THINK THAT'S WHAT SHE SAID.

CHICKEN TORTILLA LASAGNE

FAST, EASY AND DELICIOUS. GARNISH WITH SLICES OF CANTALOUPE AND HONEYDEW, ADD A GREEN SALAD AND OLE! - DINNER FOR 6.

3 CUPS SHREDDED COOKED CHICKEN	750 mL
1 CUP GRATED CHEDDAR CHEESE	250 mL
½ CUP SLICED GREEN ONIONS	125 mL
2 CUPS SOUR CREAM	500 mL
4-OZ. CAN DICED GREEN CHILIES, DRAINED	114 mL
¾ TSP. CUMIN	4 mL
12-OZ. JAR MEDIUM SALSA	341 mL
8 - 8" FLOUR TORTILLAS	8 - 20 cm
½ CUP GRATED CHEDDAR CHEESE	125 mL

PREHEAT OVEN TO 400°F. IN LARGE BOWL STIR TOGETHER CHICKEN, CHEESE, GREEN ONIONS, SOUR CREAM, CHILIES AND CUMIN. POUR 1 CUP SALSA INTO A 10" PIE PLATE. LAY 1 TORTILLA IN SALSA, COATING 1 SIDE. PLACE TORTILLA, SALSA SIDE DOWN, IN A 2-QUART ROUND CASSEROLE. SPREAD ½ CUP CHICKEN MIXTURE ON TOP OF TORTILLA. REPEAT WITH 3 MORE LAYERS OF TORTILLAS AND CHICKEN. SPREAD WITH ½ CUP SALSA. CONTINUE LAYERING TORTILLAS AND CHICKEN MIXTURE, ENDING WITH TORTILLA. TOP WITH THE SALSA (LEFTOVER FROM DIPPING THE TORTILLAS) AND CHEESE. BAKE FOR 35-40 MINUTES. LET STAND 10 MINUTES AND CUT INTO WEDGES. SERVE WITH ADDITIONAL SALSA.

IF THE WORLD IS ⅔ WATER, HOW COME OCEAN FRONT PROPERTY IS SO EXPENSIVE?

BARE-NAKED CHICKEN

FAST AND EASY!

4 BONELESS, SKINLESS CHICKEN BREAST HALVES	
SALT AND PEPPER TO TASTE	
1 TBSP. BUTTER	15 mL
½ CUP FINELY CHOPPED SHALLOTS	125 mL
¼ CUP BALSAMIC VINEGAR	60 mL
1½ CUPS CHICKEN STOCK	375 mL

SEASON CHICKEN AND BROWN IN BUTTER OVER
MEDIUM-HIGH HEAT. REDUCE HEAT AND COOK
UNTIL CHICKEN IS NO LONGER PINK IN MIDDLE. DO
NOT OVERCOOK! REMOVE TO HEATED DISH AND
SET IN WARM OVEN. ADD SHALLOTS TO PAN AND
COOK UNTIL TRANSLUCENT. ADD VINEGAR, BOIL
AND REDUCE TO GLAZE, STIRRING CONSTANTLY.
ADD CHICKEN STOCK AND BOIL UNTIL REDUCED
TO ¾ CUP. SPOON OVER CHICKEN AND RETURN
DISH TO OVEN UNTIL SERVING TIME. EXCELLENT
WITH RICE OR FETTUCCINE. SERVES 4.

6.3 GRAMS FAT PER SERVING

IT TOOK A GENIUS TO DEVELOP AN ASPIRIN BOTTLE
THAT COULDN'T BE OPENED BY A CHILD CAPABLE OF
OPERATING A VCR.

AMARETTO CHICKEN

THE VERY THING FOR THAT AGING BOTTLE OF AMARETTO IN THE LIQUOR CABINET.

2 TBSP. FLOUR	30 mL
½ TSP. SALT	2 mL
1 TSP. FRESHLY GROUND PEPPER	5 mL
1½ TSP. PAPRIKA	7 mL
1 TSP. GARLIC SALT	5 mL
6 BONELESS, SKINLESS CHICKEN BREAST HALVES	
1 TBSP. OIL	15 mL
2 TBSP. BUTTER	30 mL
1 TBSP. DIJON MUSTARD	15 mL
½ CUP FROZEN ORANGE JUICE CONCENTRATE	125 mL
¼ CUP WATER	60 mL
⅔ CUP AMARETTO	150 mL

PREHEAT OVEN TO 350°F. COMBINE FLOUR, SALT, PEPPER, PAPRIKA AND GARLIC SALT. SHAKE CHICKEN IN THIS MIXTURE. SAUTÉ CHICKEN IN OIL UNTIL BROWN AND REMOVE TO CASSEROLE. INCREASE SKILLET HEAT TO MEDIUM HIGH. MELT BUTTER; ADD MUSTARD, ORANGE JUICE, WATER AND AMARETTO. STIR CONSTANTLY UNTIL LIQUID IS REDUCED. POUR SAUCE OVER CHICKEN AND BAKE, COVERED, FOR 45 MINUTES. SERVES 6.

10.4 GRAMS FAT PER SERVING

PARADOX: TWO PH.D.S

PICTURED ON OVERLEAF

FETTUCCINE WITH ASPARAGUS AND
    SHRIMP - PAGE 117
OLIVE, ONION AND ROSEMARY FOCACCIA
    - PAGE 24

CHICKEN BREASTS ZELDA

WHY DOES DIANE ALWAYS GET THE CREDIT?

4 BONELESS, SKINLESS CHICKEN BREAST HALVES	
½ TSP. SALT	2 mL
½ TSP. FRESHLY GROUND PEPPER	2 mL
1 TBSP. VEGETABLE OIL	15 mL
1 TBSP. MARGARINE	15 mL
3 TBSP. CHOPPED GREEN ONION	45 mL
JUICE OF ½ LIME OR LEMON	
2 TBSP. BRANDY, OPTIONAL	30 mL
(ZELDA LOVES THIS)	
3 TBSP. CHOPPED FRESH PARSLEY	45 mL
2 TSP. DIJON MUSTARD	10 mL
¼ CUP CHICKEN BROTH	60 mL

PLACE CHICKEN BREAST HALVES BETWEEN SHEETS OF WAXED PAPER AND POUND SLIGHTLY WITH FLAT SIDE OF MALLET. SPRINKLE WITH SALT AND PEPPER. HEAT OIL AND MARGARINE TOGETHER IN LARGE SKILLET. COOK CHICKEN OVER MEDIUM-HIGH HEAT 4 MINUTES EACH SIDE. PLACE IN SERVING DISH AND SET IN WARM OVEN. ADD ONIONS, LIME JUICE, BRANDY, PARSLEY AND MUSTARD TO PAN. COOK 15 SECONDS, WHISKING CONSTANTLY. WHISK IN BROTH, STIRRING UNTIL SAUCE IS SMOOTH. POUR OVER WARM CHICKEN AND SERVE WITH NOODLES OR NEW POTATOES AND A SALAD. SERVES 4.

-☼- 10.5 GRAMS FAT PER SERVING

THE FUCHSIA IS THE WORLD'S MOST CAREFULLY SPELLED FLOWER.

CHICKEN MEDALLIONS WITH SPINACH

TASTES AS GOOD AS IT LOOKS.

1 ¼ LBS. SPINACH, RINSED, STEMS REMOVED	625 g
1 RED PEPPER, SLICED	
4 BONELESS, SKINESS CHICKEN BREAST HALVES	
SALT AND PEPPER TO TASTE	
1 TBSP. GRATED LEMON RIND	15 mL
1 TBSP. BUTTER	15 mL
1 TBSP. OLIVE OIL	15 mL
2 SHALLOTS, MINCED	
½ CUP CHICKEN BROTH	125 mL
¼ CUP LEMON JUICE	60 mL
1 TBSP. CHOPPED FRESH PARSLEY	15 mL
1 TBSP. CHOPPED FRESH OREGANO OR 1 TSP. (5 mL) DRIED	15 mL
1 TBSP. CAPERS	15 mL

IN SKILLET OVER MEDIUM-HIGH HEAT, SAUTÉ HALF THE SPINACH UNTIL WILTED - NO OIL REQUIRED. ADD RED PEPPER AND REMAINING SPINACH. SAUTÉ 4 MINUTES, OR UNTIL PEPPER IS TENDER CRISP AND MOST OF LIQUID EVAPORATES. REMOVE TO CASSEROLE AND KEEP WARM. PLACE CHICKEN PIECES BETWEEN WAX PAPER SHEETS AND POUND WITH MALLET TO ¾" THICKNESS. MIX SALT, PEPPER AND 1 TSP. LEMON RIND AND RUB OVER CHICKEN. IN SAME SKILLET OVER MEDIUM HIGH HEAT, MELT 1 TBSP. BUTTER IN 1 TBSP. OIL. ADD CHICKEN AND SAUTÉ 3-4 MINUTES EACH

CHICKEN MEDALLIONS WITH SPINACH

THIS RECIPE CONTINUED FROM PAGE 126.

SIDE. ARRANGE ON SPINACH AND COVER. IN DRIPPINGS OVER MEDIUM HEAT, SAUTÉ SHALLOTS 1 MINUTE. ADD CHICKEN BROTH, BRING TO BOIL, REDUCE HEAT AND ADD LEMON JUICE. WHISK IN REMAINING LEMON RIND, HERBS AND CAPERS. POUR OVER CHICKEN. SERVES 4. (SEE PICTURE ON COVER.)

 11.1 GRAMS FAT PER SERVING

THERE'S A BRAND NEW INVENTION FOR PEOPLE WHO WANT TO RELAX IN AN ATMOSPHERE OF QUIET AND TRANQUILITY. IT'S CALLED A PHONELESS CORD.

GRILLED LEMON HERB CHICKEN

BARBECUE TIME - NO GUILT, NO DISHES!

MARINADE

2 TSP. GRATED LEMON RIND	10 mL
½ CUP FRESH LEMON JUICE	125 mL
2 TBSP. OLIVE OIL	30 mL
2 TBSP. WATER	30 mL
1 TBSP. BASIL	15 mL
1 TSP. ROSEMARY	5 mL
1 TSP. THYME	5 mL
¼ TSP. FRESHLY GROUND PEPPER	1 mL
2 GARLIC CLOVES, MINCED	

6 BONELESS, SKINLESS CHICKEN BREAST HALVES

COMBINE MARINADE INGREDIENTS IN A LARGE ZIP-LOCK PLASTIC BAG. ADD CHICKEN; SEAL BAG AND MARINATE IN REFRIGERATOR FOR 8 HOURS, OCCASIONALLY TURNING BAG. SPRAY GRILL WITH COOKING OIL. COOK CHICKEN OVER MEDIUM HEAT, TURNING AND BASTING EVERY 5 MINUTES WITH RESERVED MARINADE. SERVE WITH MUSHROOMS, ONIONS, PEPPERS AND ZUCCHINI, BRUSHED WITH OLIVE OIL AND GRILLED. SERVES 6.

8.7 GRAMS FAT PER SERVING. (IF YOU WANT TO LOSE YOUR HALO, SERVE WITH FRIES!!)

PRAYING MANTIS: A STRANGE LOOKING BUG THAT SAYS GRACE BEFORE IT EATS YOUR HOUSE.

CHICKEN FINGERS

DINNER IN 20 MINUTES! YOUR CHILDREN WILL THANK YOU.

½ CUP BREAD CRUMBS	125 mL
¼ CUP GRATED PARMESAN CHEESE	60 mL
½ TSP. SALT	2 mL
1½ TSP. THYME	7 mL
1 TSP. BASIL	5 mL
2 WHOLE CHICKEN BREASTS, BONELESS, SKINLESS AND CUT INTO 1½" STRIPS	
¼ CUP BUTTER, MELTED	60 mL

PREHEAT OVEN TO 400°F. COMBINE DRY INGREDIENTS. DIP CHICKEN INTO MELTED BUTTER THEN BREAD CRUMBS. PLACE ON LIGHTLY GREASED RACK ON A COOKIE SHEET. BAKE 10 MINUTES, TURN AND BAKE 10 MINUTES MORE. DINNER'S READY! SERVE WITH HONEY MUSTARD OR PLUM DIPPING SAUCE.

THERE WILL ALWAYS BE A BATTLE BETWEEN THE SEXES BECAUSE MEN AND WOMEN WANT DIFFERENT THINGS. MEN WANT WOMEN AND WOMEN WANT MEN.

SZECHUAN CHICKEN CASSEROLE

*THIS LOOKS LIKE A LOT OF WORK - IT'S NOT!
BESIDES - IT'S A MAKE-AHEAD.*

4 BONELESS SKINLESS CHICKEN BREAST HALVES	
OR 4 CUPS (1 L) CUBED LEFTOVER CHICKEN	
2 CUPS WATER	500 mL
1 CUP UNCOOKED RICE OR	250 mL
3 CUPS (750 mL) COOKED	
2 TBSP. OIL	30 mL
1 RED PEPPER, SEEDED AND COARSELY CHOPPED	
1 GREEN PEPPER, SEEDED AND COARSELY	
CHOPPED	
1 GARLIC CLOVE, MINCED	
1" PIECE FRESH GINGER,	2.5 cm
PEELED AND MINCED	
½ TSP. FRESHLY GROUND PEPPER	2 mL
½ TSP. HOT RED PEPPER FLAKES	2 mL
¼ CUP. SOY SAUCE	60 mL
2 TBSP. SHERRY	30 mL
1 TBSP. CORNSTARCH	15 mL
1 TBSP. SESAME OIL	15 mL
1 TBSP. RICE VINEGAR	15 mL
¾ CUP CHICKEN BROTH	175 mL
¼ TSP. SALT	1 mL
¼ CUP CHOPPED, UNSALTED DRY ROASTED	60 mL
CASHEWS OR PEANUTS	
1 TSP. SESAME SEEDS	5 mL
2 GREEN ONIONS, FINELY CHOPPED	

PLACE CHICKEN IN A PAN AND COVER WITH
WATER. BRING TO BOIL, REDUCE HEAT AND
SIMMER 10 MINUTES, OR UNTIL CHICKEN IS
OPAQUE. REMOVE FROM WATER, COOL AND CUT IN

SZECHUAN CHICKEN CASSEROLE

THIS RECIPE CONTINUED FROM PAGE 130.

SMALL PIECES. COOK RICE ACCORDING TO PACKAGE DIRECTIONS. IN LARGE FRYING PAN, HEAT OIL OVER MEDIUM HEAT. ADD RED AND GREEN PEPPERS, GARLIC AND GINGER. SAUTÉ 10 MINUTES. STIR TOGETHER PEPPER, RED PEPPER FLAKES, SOY SAUCE, SHERRY, CORNSTARCH, SESAME OIL, RICE VINEGAR, CHICKEN BROTH AND SALT. ADD TO PAN AND COOK A FEW MINUTES UNTIL THICKENED. COMBINE CHICKEN, RICE AND VEGETABLES, STIRRING WELL TO BLEND. SPOON INTO LARGE CASSEROLE OR A 9" X 13" PAN. (THE CASSEROLE CAN BE REFRIGERATED OVERNIGHT, BUT SPRINKLE WITH ¼ CUP CHICKEN BROTH BEFORE COOKING.) BAKE AT 350°F FOR 25 MINUTES, OR UNTIL HEATED THROUGH. TO SERVE, COMBINE NUTS, SESAME SEEDS AND GREEN ONIONS AND SPRINKLE OVER TOP. SERVES 6.

12.9 GRAMS FAT PER SERVING

10.2 GRAMS FAT PER SERVING WITHOUT CASHEWS

YOUNG WOMAN TO FRIEND: "I THOUGHT ABOUT A MEANINGFUL RELATIONSHIP WITH BOB, BUT THEN I FOUND OUT IT INVOLVED COOKING."

THIGH CHICKEN

A MILD-FLAVORED CASSEROLE, BUT IF YOU REALLY WANT TO "THAI" ONE ON - ADD MORE HOT CHILI SAUCE.

2 LBS. CHICKEN THIGHS, SKIN REMOVED	1 Kg
2 TBSP. VEGETABLE OIL	30 mL
1 MEDIUM ONION, CHOPPED	
1 GARLIC CLOVE, MINCED	
1 TSP. CORIANDER	5 mL
1 TSP. CUMIN	5 mL
1 TSP. SALT	5 mL
2 TSP. GRATED FRESH GINGER	10 mL
2-3 TSP. SWEET HOT ORIENTAL CHILI SAUCE	10-15 mL
2 TBSP. SOY SAUCE	30 mL
2 TBSP. PEANUT BUTTER	30 mL
14-OZ. CAN COCONUT MILK	398 mL
1 TSP. GRATED LIME RIND	5 mL
JUICE OF 1 LIME	

IN A DUTCH OVEN, HEAT OIL AND BROWN CHICKEN (15 MINUTES). SET ASIDE IN A LARGE CASSEROLE. SAUTÉ ONION AND GARLIC AND COOK UNTIL TENDER. STIR IN CORIANDER, CUMIN, SALT, GINGER, CHILI SAUCE, SOY SAUCE AND PEANUT BUTTER. ADD COCONUT MILK AND STIR TO BLEND. POUR MIXTURE OVER CHICKEN, COVER AND COOK 1 HOUR AT 325°F. JUST BEFORE SERVING, STIR IN LIME RIND AND JUICE. SERVE OVER RICE.

FORUM: TWO-UM AND TWO-UM.

PHEASANT CASSEROLE

IF YOUR HUNTER BRINGS HOME THE BIRDS, YOU CAN PHIX HIS PHEASANTS.

½ CUP FLOUR	125 mL
¼ TSP. SAGE	1 mL
½ TSP. SALT	2 mL
SEASONED PEPPER TO TASTE	
4 PHEASANT BREASTS, CUT INTO BITE-SIZED PIECES	
2 TBSP. VEGETABLE OIL	30 mL
4 GREEN ONIONS, CHOPPED	
½ GREEN PEPPER, CUT IN STRIPS	
½ RED PEPPER, CUT IN STRIPS	
2 CELERY STALKS, CHOPPED	
1 CUP SLICED MUSHROOMS	250 mL
2 - 10-OZ. CANS MUSHROOM SOUP	2 - 284 mL
1 CUP MILK	250 mL
½ CUP WHITE WINE	125 mL

PREHEAT OVEN TO 325°F. MIX FLOUR AND SEASONINGS TOGETHER. COAT PHEASANT PIECES WITH FLOUR MIXTURE AND BROWN IN HOT OIL. PLACE IN CASSEROLE WITH VEGETABLES. MIX MUSHROOM SOUP, MILK AND WINE AND POUR OVER MIXTURE. BAKE AT LEAST 1 HOUR, STIRRING OCCASIONALLY. ADD MORE WINE IF SAUCE BECOMES TOO THICK. SERVES 4

NEVER SLAP A MAN WHO CHEWS TOBACCO.

PHEASANT PIE

THE BROTH

2 PHEASANTS
6 CUPS WATER — 1.5 L
1 TSP. SALT — 5 mL
1 MEDIUM ONION, PEELED AND CUT IN HALF
4 CLOVES
2 BAY LEAVES
10 PEPPERCORNS

THE SAUCE

3 TBSP. BUTTER — 45 mL
1/4 CUP FLOUR — 60 mL
2 CUPS PHEASANT BROTH — 500 mL
1/2 CUP WHIPPING CREAM — 125 mL
3 MEDIUM CARROTS, SLICED
8 OZ. MUSHROOMS, QUARTERED — 250 g
SALT AND PEPPER TO TASTE
1 CUP PEAS, FRESH OR FROZEN — 250 mL
7-OZ. PKG. FROZEN PUFF PASTRY — 200 g

TO MAKE BROTH: CUT PHEASANTS INTO QUARTERS, WASH AND PLACE IN LARGE POT (DON'T FORGET THE NECKS!). ADD WATER AND SALT AND BRING TO A BOIL. ADD ONION, CLOVES, BAY LEAVES AND PEPPERCORNS. SIMMER 1 HOUR, OR UNTIL MEAT IS TENDER. REMOVE MEAT, SET ASIDE AND LET COOL. STRAIN BROTH.

TO MAKE SAUCE: MELT BUTTER IN SAUCEPAN OVER MEDIUM HEAT. ADD FLOUR AND COOK FOR A FEW MINUTES STIRRING CONSTANTLY. WHISK IN

PHEASANT PIE

THIS RECIPE CONTINUED FROM PAGE 134.

BROTH AND BRING TO BOIL. ADD CREAM, CARROTS AND MUSHROOMS AND SIMMER FOR 15 MINUTES. SPRINKLE WITH SALT AND PEPPER. ADD PEAS AND REMOVE FROM HEAT.

REMOVE SKIN AND BONE THE PHEASANTS. CUT MEAT INTO PIECES AND PLACE IN A 4-QUART CASSEROLE. POUR SAUCE OVER PHEASANT. THAW AND ROLL OUT PUFF PASTRY TO 1/8" THICKNESS. COVER CASSEROLE, MAKE SEVERAL SLASHES ON TOP AND PLACE IN 400°F OVEN FOR 30 MINUTES OR UNTIL PASTRY IS GOLDEN BROWN. SERVE WITH RICE OR BOILED NEW POTATOES. SERVES 4-6 HUNTERS AND STAY-AT-HOMES.

THE PRAIRIE DWELLER'S VERSION OF "WHY DID THE CHICKEN CROSS THE ROAD?" TO PROVE TO THE GOPHERS THAT IT COULD BE DONE.

POACHED SALMON WITH PIQUANT SAUCE AND VEGGIES

A DELICIOUS DINNER FOR 4. SERVE WITH STEAMED RICE.

PIQUANT SAUCE

3 TBSP. LOW-FAT MAYONNAISE	45 mL
1 TBSP. CHOPPED FRESH DILL,	15 mL
OR 1 TSP. (5 mL) DRY DILL	
1 TBSP. SKIM MILK	15 mL
1 TBSP. CHOPPED CAPERS	15 mL
2 TSP. JUICE FROM CAPERS	10 mL
1½ TSP. DIJON MUSTARD	7 mL
¼ TSP. GRATED LEMON RIND	1 mL

SALMON

1 LB. SALMON FILLET	500 g
3 CUPS WATER	750 mL
1 SMALL LEMON, THINLY SLICED	
2 TSP. INSTANT CHICKEN BOUILLON POWDER	10 mL

VEGETABLES

1½ CUPS WATER	375 mL
1 TSP. INSTANT CHICKEN BOUILLON	5 mL
3 MEDIUM CARROTS, SLICED INTO MATCHSTICKS	
1 MEDIUM ZUCCHINI (UNPEELED), SLICED INTO	
MATCHSTICKS	
CHOPPED FRESH DILL FOR GARNISH	

TO PREPARE PIQUANT SAUCE: COMBINE INGREDIENTS IN SMALL BOWL AND SET ASIDE.

A FLASHLIGHT IS SOMETHING YOU CARRY DEAD BATTERIES IN.

POACHED SALMON WITH PIQUANT SAUCE AND VEGGIES

THIS RECIPE CONTINUED FROM PAGE 136.

TO POACH SALMON: REMOVE ANY SMALL BONES WITH TWEEZERS AND CUT SALMON INTO 4 PIECES. IN LARGE SKILLET, BRING 3 CUPS WATER TO A BOIL. ADD LEMON SLICES AND CHICKEN BOUILLON. COVER AND SIMMER FOR 5 MINUTES. ADD SALMON AND HEAT TO BOILING. REDUCE HEAT TO LOW; COVER AND SIMMER 8-10 MINUTES, UNTIL FISH FLAKES EASILY WHEN TESTED WITH FORK.

TO PREPARE VEGGIES: WHILE FISH IS POACHING, HEAT WATER AND BOUILLON TO BOILING. ADD CARROTS, REDUCE HEAT TO LOW, COVER AND SIMMER 2 MINUTES. ADD ZUCCHINI, HEAT TO BOILING, COVER AND SIMMER 2 MINUTES LONGER OR UNTIL VEGETABLES ARE TENDER-CRISP. DRAIN. ARRANGE SALMON, STEAMED RICE, AND VEGETABLES ON A WARM PLATTER. GARNISH WITH SAUCE & DILL.

(PICTURED ON PAGE 141.)

16.2 GRAMS OF FAT (THE GOOD FAT!) PER SERVING

AS LONG AS THERE IS MATHEMATICS, THERE WILL ALWAYS BE PRAYER IN SCHOOLS.

ORANGE ROUGHIE POLYNESIAN

QUICK AND DELICIOUS.

1½ LBS. ORANGE ROUGHIE	750 g
(RED SNAPPER IS GOOD TOO)	
3 TBSP. LIGHT SOY SAUCE	45 mL
2 TBSP. RICE VINEGAR OR DRY SHERRY	30 mL
2 TBSP. LEMON JUICE	30 mL
1 TBSP. OLIVE OIL	15 mL
1 GREEN ONION, CHOPPED	
2 TSP. CHOPPED GINGER	10 mL

CUT FISH INTO SERVING-SIZED PIECES AND SET ASIDE. MIX SOY SAUCE, RICE VINEGAR, LEMON JUICE, OLIVE OIL, GREEN ONION AND GINGER IN A SHALLOW DISH. PLACE FISH IN MARINADE. LET STAND 30 MINUTES, TURNING ONCE. PLACE FISH ON PAN UNDER PREHEATED BROILER FOR 2-3 MINUTES. TURN AND BROIL 2 MORE MINUTES, UNTIL FISH IS OPAQUE. SERVE OVER RICE. SERVES 4.

 6.4 GRAMS OF FAT PER SERVING

IN SPITE OF THE COST OF LIVING, IT'S STILL POPULAR.

RED SNAPPER PARMESAN

A HALO IN A HURRY.

3/4 LB. RED SNAPPER	365 g
1 TBSP. LEMON JUICE	15 mL
2 TBSP. GRATED PARMESAN CHEESE	30 mL
2 TBSP. SKIM MILK YOGURT	30 mL
2 TBSP. LOW-FAT MAYONNAISE	30 mL
2 TBSP. FINELY CHOPPED GREEN ONION	30 mL
2 TBSP. CHOPPED PIMIENTO	30 mL
1/2 TSP. DRIED DILL	2 mL

PLACE FILLETS IN BAKING DISH AND BRUSH WITH LEMON JUICE. LET STAND 20 MINUTES. PREHEAT BROILER. COMBINE REMAINING INGREDIENTS AND BROIL FILLETS 6-8 MINUTES UNTIL FLAKY. SPOON MIXTURE OVER FILLETS AND BROIL ANOTHER 3 MINUTES. SERVE WITH RICE. SERVES 2.

 9.9 GRAMS OF FAT PER SERVING

WHY IS IT THAT WHEN WE BOUNCE A CHEQUE, THE BANK CHARGES US MORE OF WHAT THEY ALREADY KNOW WE DON'T HAVE ANY OF?

SHRIMP, RICE AND ARTICHOKE CASSEROLE

GREAT MAKE-AHEAD DISH FOR 6-8 GUESTS.

1 MEDIUM ONION, CHOPPED	
2 STALKS CELERY, CHOPPED	
3 GARLIC CLOVES, MINCED	
2 GREEN PEPPERS, CHOPPED	
2 BAY LEAVES	
1/4 CUP BUTTER	60 mL
3 LBS. SHRIMP, BOILED, PEELED AND DEVEINED	1.5 kg
4 CUPS COOKED RICE	1 L
1/2 CUP TOMATO SAUCE	125 mL
1 CUP WHIPPING CREAM	250 mL
3/4 TSP. CAYENNE PEPPER	3 mL
SALT TO TASTE	
2 - 14-OZ. CANS ARTICHOKE HEARTS (12-14 COUNT), DRAINED AND HALVED	2 - 398 mL
1 1/2 CUPS GRATED CHEDDAR OR SWISS CHEESE	375 mL

SAUTÉ ONION, CELERY, GARLIC, PEPPERS AND BAY LEAVES IN BUTTER UNTIL ONION IS SOFT. DISCARD GARLIC CLOVES. ADD COOKED SHRIMP AND RICE, STIRRING UNTIL HOT. ADD TOMATO SAUCE, CREAM, CAYENNE, SALT AND ARTICHOKES. STIR WELL. REMOVE BAY LEAVES. POUR INTO 9" X 13" GLASS BAKING DISH. IF CASSEROLE IS NOT BAKED IMMEDIATELY, COVER AND REFRIGERATE UNTIL READY TO BAKE. BEFORE BAKING, SPRINKLE WITH CHEESE. COVER AND BAKE AT 350°F FOR 30 MINUTES, OR UNTIL HEATED THROUGH.

PICTURED ON OVERLEAF

POACHED SALMON WITH PIQUANT SAUCE
AND VEGGIES - PAGE 136

LAYERED TUNA CASSEROLE

DOWN-HOME COOKIN'! A TASTY FAMILY CASSEROLE THAT TAKES ABOUT 20 MINUTES TO PREPARE, 30 MINUTES TO COOK AND HOW LONG IT TAKES TO EAT IS UP TO YOU!

2 - 6½-oz. CANS CHUNK-STYLE TUNA, PACKED IN WATER	2 - 184 g
3 CUPS UNCOOKED EGG NOODLES	750 mL
½ CUP CHOPPED CELERY	125 mL
⅓ CUP FINELY CHOPPED GREEN ONIONS	75 mL
⅔ CUP 7% SOUR CREAM	150 mL
2 TSP. DRY MUSTARD	10 mL
½ CUP LIGHT MAYONNAISE	125 mL
½ TSP. THYME	2 mL
¼ TSP. SALT	1 mL
1 MEDIUM ZUCCHINI, SLICED	
½ CUP GRATED SKIM MILK MOZZARELLA CHEESE	125 mL
½ CUP GRATED LIGHT CHEDDAR CHEESE	125 mL
1 TOMATO, CHOPPED (OPTIONAL)	

DRAIN AND FLAKE TUNA. SET ASIDE. COOK NOODLES ACCORDING TO PACKAGE DIRECTIONS. DRAIN, RINSE IN HOT WATER. COMBINE TUNA, NOODLES, CELERY AND ONIONS. BLEND TOGETHER SOUR CREAM, MUSTARD, MAYONNAISE, THYME AND SALT AND MIX INTO TUNA MIXTURE. SPOON HALF OF THIS MIXTURE INTO A GREASED 2-QUART CASSEROLE. TOP WITH HALF THE ZUCCHINI. REPEAT LAYERS AND TOP WITH GRATED CHEESES. BAKE AT 350°F FOR 30-40 MINUTES. TOP WITH CHOPPED TOMATO. SERVES 8.

11.1 GRAMS FAT PER SERVING

ORANGE STIR-FRIED SHRIMP

SERVE WITH ORANGE RICE (PAGE 146).

MARINADE

1 GARLIC CLOVE, MINCED	
1 TSP. GRATED ORANGE RIND	5 mL
1/4 TSP. HOT RED PEPPER FLAKES	1 mL
1 TSP. SOY SAUCE	5 mL
1 TSP. SESAME OIL	5 mL
1 LB. SHRIMP, SHELLED AND DEVEINED	500 g

SAUCE

1/2 CUP ORANGE JUICE	125 mL
2 TBSP. SOY SAUCE	30 mL
1 TBSP. HONEY OR SUGAR	15 mL
2 TSP. CORNSTARCH	10 mL
1 TSP. SESAME OIL	5 mL

STIR-FRY

1 TBSP. OIL	15 mL
1 TBSP. FINELY CHOPPED FRESH GINGER	15 mL
1 GARLIC CLOVE, MINCED	
1/2 LB. GREEN BEANS, SLICED	250 g
1 1/2 CUPS MUSHROOMS, SLICED	375 mL
1 RED PEPPER, CUT IN STRIPS	
3 SCALLIONS OR GREEN ONIONS, SLICED DIAGONALLY	

TO PREPARE MARINADE: IN LARGE BOWL BLEND ALL MARINADE INGREDIENTS. ADD SHRIMP, COVER AND REFRIGERATE 1 HOUR.

ORANGE STIR-FRIED SHRIMP

THIS RECIPE CONTINUED FROM PAGE 144.

TO MAKE SAUCE: IN A SMALL BOWL, MIX INGREDIENTS UNTIL SMOOTH AND SET ASIDE.

TO STIR-FRY: HEAT WOK OR LARGE FRYING PAN UNTIL HOT. ADD OIL, GINGER AND GARLIC AND STIR-FRY 20 SECONDS. ADD GREEN BEANS, STIR-FRY 3 MINUTES. ADD MUSHROOMS AND RED PEPPER AND STIR-FRY 3 MINUTES MORE. ADD SHRIMP AND MARINADE; STIR-FRY 4 MINUTES, OR JUST UNTIL SHRIMP TURNS PINK. STIR SAUCE. ADD SCALLIONS; STIR INTO SHRIMP UNTIL MIXTURE IS COATED AND SAUCE THICKENS. (AREN'T YOU JUST EXHAUSTED??) SERVES 4.

8.2 GRAMS FAT PER SERVING

WITH ORANGE RICE - 12 GRAMS OF FAT PER SERVING

LIVING ON A BUDGET IS THE SAME AS LIVING BEYOND YOUR MEANS EXCEPT YOU HAVE A RECORD OF IT.

ORANGE RICE

SERVE WITH ORANGE STIR-FRIED SHRIMP
(PAGE 144).

1 TBSP. VEGETABLE OIL	15 mL
1 TSP. GRATED ORANGE RIND	5 mL
1 CUP LONG-GRAIN RICE	250 mL
1 TSP. SALT	5 mL
1¾ CUPS WATER	425 mL

HEAT OIL IN A SAUCEPAN. ADD ORANGE RIND AND
RICE. SAUTÉ 2 MINUTES, OR UNTIL RICE TURNS
MILKY WHITE. ADD SALT AND WATER. HEAT TO
BOILING, STIR TO MIX, COVER. OVER MEDIUM-HEAT,
COOK RICE 25 MINUTES, OR UNTIL LIQUID IS
ABSORBED. REMOVE PAN FROM HEAT. LET STAND
COVERED 10 MINUTES BEFORE SERVING. SERVES 4.

3.8 GRAMS OF FAT PER SERVING

THE COMPANY ACCOUNTANT IS SHY AND RETIRING.
HE'S SHY A QUARTER OF A MILLION DOLLARS, SO HE'S
RETIRING.

VEAL WITH ARTICHOKES

¾ LB. VEAL SCALLOPINI	365 g
2 TBSP. BUTTER	30 mL
3 CUPS THICKLY SLICED MUSHROOMS	750 mL
½ CUP CHICKEN BROTH	125 mL
2 TBSP. BRANDY (OPTIONAL)	30 mL
14-OZ. CAN ARTICHOKE HEARTS, DRAINED AND QUARTERED	398 mL
½ TSP. THYME	2 mL
¼ TSP. FRESHLY GROUND PEPPER	1 mL
PINCH OF SALT	
¼ CUP CHOPPED FRESH CHIVES OR GREEN ONIONS	60 mL

CUT VEAL IN 2" X 3" PIECES. OVER MEDIUM-HIGH HEAT, MELT 1 TBSP. BUTTER IN LARGE FRYING PAN. ADD HALF THE VEAL AND COOK UNTIL LIGHTLY BROWNED. PLACE VEAL IN OVENPROOF DISH. REPEAT WITH REMAINING BUTTER AND VEAL. ADD MUSHROOMS TO PAN AND SAUTÉ UNTIL BROWNED. STIR IN BROTH AND BRANDY. INCREASE HEAT AND BRING TO BOIL. ADD ARTICHOKES AND SPRINKLE WITH SEASONINGS. STIR UNTIL ARTICHOKES ARE HOT. SPRINKLE WITH CHIVES AND POUR OVER VEAL. SERVE WITH NOODLES. SERVES 4.

7.9 GRAMS FAT PER SERVING

THE IDEAL PLACE FOR A PICNIC IS USUALLY A LITTLE FURTHER ON.

BEEF TENDERLOIN WITH PEPPERCORN SAUCE

LIGHT THE CANDLES, POUR THE WINE, ISN'T ENTERTAINING JUST DIVINE?

THE SAUCE

2 TBSP. BUTTER	30 mL
¼ CUP CHOPPED SHALLOTS	60 mL
2 TBSP. GREEN PEPPERCORNS (CANNED)	30 mL
¼ CUP BRANDY	60 mL
1½ CUPS WHIPPING CREAM	375 mL
1 TBSP. STEAK SAUCE OR BARBECUE SAUCE	15 mL
2 TBSP. CHOPPED FRESH PARSLEY	30 mL

1 BEEF TENDERLOIN
      APPROXIMATELY 2½ LBS. (1.25 kg)
VEGETABLE OIL
SALT AND COARSELY GROUND PEPPER

FOR THE SAUCE: MELT BUTTER IN SAUCEPAN, ADD SHALLOTS AND PEPPERCORNS AND SAUTÉ UNTIL SOFT. ADD BRANDY AND BRING TO BOIL. ADD CREAM AND STEAK SAUCE AND SIMMER UNTIL SLIGHTLY THICKENED - ABOUT 5 MINUTES. ADD PARSLEY AND SET ASIDE.

TO PREPARE MEAT: BRUSH TENDERLOIN WITH OIL AND SEASON WITH SALT AND PEPPER. BAKE AT 450°F FOR 30 MINUTES FOR MEDIUM BEEF. SLICE AND SERVE WITH WARMED PEPPERCORN SAUCE.

LIFE IS LIKE A DOGSLED TEAM. IF YOU AIN'T THE LEAD DOG, THE SCENERY NEVER CHANGES.

GINGER-GARLIC FLANK STEAK

LEAN, TENDER AND JUICY - A SUPERB BARBECUED STEAK. SERVE WITH STIR-FRIED VEGETABLES AND RICE.

1½-2 LBS. FLANK STEAK	750 g-1kg

MARINADE

3 TBSP. BROWN SUGAR	45 mL
¼ CUP SALT-REDUCED SOY SAUCE	60 mL
¼ CUP ORANGE JUICE	60 mL
½ CUP SHERRY	125 mL
1 TBSP. MINCED FRESH GINGER	15 mL
2 GARLIC CLOVES, MINCED	

MAKE SHALLOW DIAGONAL SLASHES ACROSS THE STEAK (ALL THE BETTER TO TENDERIZE) AND A COUPLE OF CUTS ON THE EDGES (ALL THE BETTER NOT TO CURL, M'DEAR). MIX MARINADE INGREDIENTS TOGETHER AND PLACE IN A ZIPLOCK BAG WITH THE STEAK. STORE OVERNIGHT IN THE REFRIGERATOR, TURNING ONCE OR TWICE (BUT DON'T GET OUT OF BED TO DO IT). SPRAY BARBECUE WITH COOKING SPRAY. GRILL APPROXIMATELY 4 MINUTES EACH SIDE FOR MEDIUM RARE. SLICE ACROSS THE GRAIN IN ¼" STRIPS. SERVES 4.

12.5 GRAMS FAT PER SERVING

IF PEOPLE WERE NOT MEANT TO HAVE A MIDNIGHT SNACK, WHY DID THEY PUT A LIGHT IN THE REFRIGERATOR?

BULGOGI (KOREAN STIR-FRY)

1½ LBS. SIRLOIN STEAK	750 g
2 TBSP. SUGAR	30 mL
1 TSP. PEPPER	5 mL
1 TBSP. SESAME SEEDS	15 mL
2 TSP. SESAME SEED OIL	10 mL
2 TBSP. CHOPPED GREEN ONION	30 mL
3-5 GARLIC CLOVES, CHOPPED (IT'S YOUR LIFE)	
2 TBSP. SOY SAUCE	30 mL
1 TSP. CHOPPED FRESH GINGER	5 mL
2 TBSP. RESERVED PEACH JUICE	30 mL
14-OZ. CAN SLICED PEACHES, DRAINED	398 mL

SLICE BEEF IN THIN STRIPS - 3" LONG. MIX BEEF
WITH SUGAR AND SET IN REFRIGERATOR FOR AT
LEAST ½ HOUR. MIX REMAINING INGREDIENTS,
EXCLUDING PEACHES. ADD TO BEEF AND SUGAR
MIXTURE. MIX WELL. STIR-FRY. SERVE WITH SNOW
PEAS, STEAMED RICE AND SLICED PEACHES.
SERVES 4.

TELEVISION REMOTE CONTROLS ENCOURAGE COUCH
POTATOES TO EXERCISE THEIR OPTIONS WHILE
BROADENING THEIR BASE.

MEXICAN ROUNDUP STEAK

A TASTY VARIATION OF SWISS STEAK. SERVE WITH LOTS OF MASHED POTATOES.

1 LB. ROUND OR SIRLOIN STEAK	500 g
1 TBSP. OLIVE OIL	15 mL
2 ONIONS, SLICED	
2 GARLIC CLOVES, MINCED	
1 CUP MILD OR MEDIUM SALSA	250 mL
1 CUP BEEF BROTH	250 mL
3 TBSP. LIME JUICE	45 mL
1 TSP. CUMIN	5 mL

POUND STEAK WITH MALLET AND CUT INTO 4 PIECES. IN A DUTCH OVEN, BROWN STEAK IN OIL OVER MEDIUM-HIGH HEAT. ADD ONIONS AND GARLIC AND COOK UNTIL SOFT. SET ASIDE. IN A SAUCEPAN, COMBINE SALSA, BROTH, LIME JUICE AND CUMIN. BRING TO BOIL AND POUR OVER STEAK, STIRRING TO LOOSEN BROWN BITS ON BOTTOM OF PAN. COVER AND BAKE AT 300°F FOR 1½ TO 2 HOURS. STIR OCCASIONALLY, ADDING MORE BROTH IF NECESSARY.

 12.8 GRAMS FAT PER SERVING

FAD DIETS ARE SO POPULAR YOU'D THINK THE SLEEK WERE GOING TO INHERIT THE EARTH.

TOURTIÈRE WITH MUSHROOM SAUCE

A CHRISTMAS EVE TRADITION AND A PERFECT GIFT. SAVE TIME AND YOUR SANITY - MAKE AHEAD AND FREEZE.

ENOUGH PASTRY FOR 3, 2-CRUST PIES

1½ LBS. LEAN GROUND PORK	750 g
1½ LBS. LEAN GROUND BEEF	750 g
1½ CUPS FINELY CHOPPED ONION	375 mL
1 TSP. THYME	5 mL
1 TSP. SAGE	5 mL
1 TSP. DRY MUSTARD	5 mL
2 TSP. SALT	10 mL
½ CUP CHOPPED FRESH PARSLEY	125 mL
2 GARLIC CLOVES, MINCED	
PEPPER TO TASTE	
1 CUP WATER	250 mL
1 CUP BREAD CRUMBS	250 mL
OR 2 CUPS (500 mL) MASHED POTATOES	

MUSHROOM SAUCE

2 TBSP. BUTTER	30 mL
3 CUPS SLICED MUSHROOMS	750 mL
½ CUP SLICED ONIONS	125 mL
2 TBSP. BUTTER	30 mL
2 TSP. FLOUR	10 mL
1 CUP BEEF BROTH	250 mL
½ CUP DRY RED WINE	125 mL

TO MAKE PIES: IN FRYING PAN, LIGHTLY BROWN MEAT. DRAIN OFF FAT. ADD ONION AND STIR IN SEASONINGS. ADD WATER, COVER AND SIMMER 15 MINUTES, OR UNTIL MOST OF LIQUID IS ABSORBED BUT MIXTURE IS STILL MOIST.

TOURTIÈRE WITH MUSHROOM SAUCE

THIS RECIPE CONTINUED FROM PAGE 152.

ADD BREAD CRUMBS. LET COOL. SPOON MIXTURE INTO PASTRY-LINED 9" PIE PLATES. COVER WITH TOP CRUSTS, SEAL AND FLUTE EDGES. MAY BE FROZEN AT THIS POINT. CUT SLASHES ON TOP TO RELEASE STEAM. BAKE 425°F FOR 15 MINUTES, REDUCE HEAT TO 350°F AND BAKE 30 MINUTES, OR UNTIL WELL BROWNED. THIS RECIPE CAN ALSO BE MADE AS AN APPETIZER USING TART SHELLS.

TO MAKE MUSHROOM SAUCE: SAUTÉ MUSHROOMS AND ONIONS IN BUTTER FOR 10 MINUTES. REMOVE TO PLATE. MELT BUTTER AND BLEND FLOUR AND A FEW TABLESPOONS OF BEEF BROTH INTO PAN JUICES. STIR IN REMAINING BEEF BROTH AND WINE. BRING TO A BOIL UNTIL MIXTURE THICKENS. ADD MUSHROOMS AND ONIONS BACK INTO SAUCE. SERVE WARM WITH TOURTIÈRE.

IT TOOK HIM 6 MONTHS TO SING "NIGHT AND DAY". HE WAS AN ESKIMO.

SKILLET CHILI PIE WITH CORN BREAD TOPPING

CHILI MIXTURE

1 CUP CHOPPED ONION	250 mL
1 CUP CHOPPED GREEN PEPPER	250 mL
½ LB. LEAN GROUND BEEF	250 g
1 CUP KERNEL CORN, DRAINED	250 mL
2 TSP. CHILI POWDER	10 mL
1 TSP. CUMIN	5 mL
½ TSP. SUGAR	2 mL
½ TSP. GARLIC POWDER	2 mL
¾ CUP WATER	175 mL
14-OZ. CAN PINTO BEANS, DRAINED	398 mL
14-OZ. CAN STEWED TOMATOES	398 mL
5½-OZ. CAN TOMATO PASTE	156 g
4-OZ. CAN CHOPPED GREEN CHILIES, DRAINED	114 g

TOPPING

½ CUP FLOUR	125 mL
½ CUP CORNMEAL	125 mL
1 TSP. BAKING POWDER	5 mL
⅛ TSP. SALT	0.5 mL
½ CUP BUTTERMILK	125 mL
1 EGG WHITE, SLIGHTLY BEATEN	

TO MAKE CHILI: COOK ONION, GREEN PEPPER AND GROUND BEEF IN A LARGE OVENPROOF SKILLET OVER MEDIUM HEAT UNTIL MEAT IS BROWNED AND CRUMBLY. DRAIN WELL ON PAPER TOWEL AND SET ASIDE. WIPE DRIPPINGS FROM SKILLET WITH A PAPER TOWEL. RETURN MEAT MIXTURE TO SKILLET AND ADD REMAINING INGREDIENTS.

SKILLET CHILI PIE WITH CORN BREAD TOPPING

THIS RECIPE CONTINUED FROM PAGE 154.

BRING TO BOIL, COVER, REDUCE HEAT TO MEDIUM LOW AND COOK 10 MINUTES, STIRRING OCCASIONALLY. REMOVE FROM HEAT AND SET ASIDE.

TO MAKE CORN BREAD: COMBINE DRY INGREDIENTS IN A BOWL. COMBINE BUTTERMILK AND EGG WHITE AND ADD TO DRY INGREDIENTS, STIRRING UNTIL MOISTENED. SPOON EVENLY OVER MEAT MIXTURE. BAKE AT 400°F FOR 13 MINUTES, OR UNTIL TOOTHPICK INSERTED IN CENTER COMES OUT CLEAN. SERVES 5.

— ⬭ — 8 GRAMS OF FAT PER SERVING

IMMORTAL WORDS:

KNOW THYSELF - SOCRATES

TO THINE OWN SELF BE TRUE - SHAKESPEARE

NEVER WASH WHITES WITH COLORS - MOM

EL GRANDE STACKO TORTA!

2 LBS. LEAN GROUND BEEF	1 kg
1 ONION, CHOPPED	
1 GARLIC CLOVE, MINCED	
2 TBSP. CHILI POWDER	30 mL
3 CUPS TOMATO SAUCE	750 mL
1 TSP. SUGAR	5 mL
1 TSP. SALT	5 mL
½ CUP SLICED BLACK OLIVES	125 mL
2 - 4-oz. CANS CHOPPED GREEN CHILIES	2 - 114 g
SLICED JALAPEÑO PEPPER (OPTIONAL)	
2 CUPS RICOTTA CHEESE	500 mL
1 EGG, BEATEN	
2 CUPS GRATED MONTEREY JACK CHEESE	500 mL
12 SOFT CORN TORTILLAS	
1 CUP GRATED CHEDDAR CHEESE	250 mL

TOPPINGS

CHOPPED GREEN ONIONS, SOUR CREAM, SALSA.

BROWN MEAT AND DRAIN. ADD ONIONS AND GARLIC; SAUTÉ UNTIL SOFT. SPRINKLE WITH CHILI AND MIX WELL. ADD TOMATO SAUCE, SUGAR, SALT, OLIVES, CHILIES AND JALAPEÑO. SIMMER 15 MINUTES. BEAT RICOTTA AND EGG TOGETHER. SET ASIDE. IN A 9" X 13" PAN, LAYER ⅓ MEAT MIXTURE, ½ THE MONTEREY JACK CHEESE, ½ THE RICOTTA FOLLOWED BY ½ THE TORTILLAS. REPEAT PROCESS ENDING WITH MEAT SAUCE ON TOP. SPRINKLE WITH CHEDDAR CHEESE. BAKE AT 350°F FOR 30 MINUTES. SERVE TOPPINGS AT TABLE IN INDIVIDUAL BOWLS. SERVES 8.

CASSEROLE FOR A COLD NIGHT

1 LB. LEAN GROUND BEEF	500 g
7½-OZ. CAN TOMATO SAUCE	213 g
1 GARLIC CLOVE, MINCED	
SALT AND PEPPER TO TASTE	
2 TSP. SUGAR	10 mL
14-OZ. CAN TOMATOES	398 mL
3 CUPS BROAD EGG NOODLES, COOKED AND DRAINED	750 mL
4 OZ. LIGHT CREAM CHEESE, CUBED	125 mL
1 CUP 7% SOUR CREAM	250 mL
6 GREEN ONIONS, CHOPPED	
1½ CUPS GRATED LIGHT CHEDDAR CHEESE	375 mL

BROWN MEAT AND DRAIN. ADD TOMATO SAUCE, GARLIC, SALT, PEPPER, SUGAR AND TOMATOES. COVER AND SIMMER OVER LOW HEAT FOR 45 MINUTES. PREHEAT OVEN TO 350°F. COMBINE HOT NOODLES WITH CUBED CREAM CHEESE. STIR TO MELT CHEESE. ADD SOUR CREAM AND GREEN ONIONS. IN A GREASED 3-QUART BAKING DISH, LAYER MEAT SAUCE, NOODLE MIXTURE AND CHEDDAR CHEESE ALTERNATELY. BAKE UNCOVERED FOR 30 MINUTES. SERVES 6.

EVEN A MOSQUITO DOESN'T GET A SLAP ON THE BACK UNTIL HE STARTS TO WORK.

SOUVLAKI

DON'T THROW THE PLATES - THROW A PARTY!

MAKE THESE LAMB KABOBS AND ASK 6 FRIENDS TO BRING: SPANAKOPITA FOR AN APPETIZER ("GRAND SLAM", PAGE 58), GREEK SALAD ("WINNERS", PAGE 70), AND FOR DESSERT (THIS ISN'T GREEK, BUT IT'S DARN GOOD), SERVE ICE BOX PUDDING ("BEST OF BRIDGE", PAGE 170).

4 LBS. LAMB (LEG OR SHOULDER)	2 kg
1 TSP. SEASONED SALT	5 mL
1 TSP. PEPPER	5 mL
1 TSP. OREGANO	5 mL
½ CUP OLIVE OIL	125 mL
JUICE OF 2 SMALL LEMONS	

CUT MEAT INTO 1½" CUBES AND PLACE ON SKEWERS. SEASON WITH SALT AND PEPPER. BARBECUE OR BROIL OVER MEDIUM HEAT, BASTING WITH MIXTURE OF OREGANO, OIL AND LEMON JUICE, TURNING TO BROWN EVENLY (ABOUT 10 MINUTES). KEEP WARM UNTIL SERVING TIME. SERVE WITH TZATZIKI (PAGE 41) AND WARM PITA BREAD. SERVES 6.

DID YOU HEAR ABOUT THE HUNTER WHO FOLLOWED SOME TRACKS INTO A CAVE.....AND SHOT A TRAIN?

MOUTH-WATERING AROMAS FROM YOUR KITCHEN AND KUDOS FROM YOUR COMPANY. SERVE OVER COCONUT RICE (PAGE 90).

3 LBS. BONELESS LAMB (LEG OR SHOULDER)	1.5 kg
3 TBSP. OLIVE OIL	45 mL
4 MEDIUM ONIONS, CHOPPED	
4 GARLIC CLOVES, MINCED	
28-OZ. CAN TOMATOES	796 mL
5½-OZ. CAN TOMATO PASTE	156 mL
1 CUP DRY RED WINE	250 mL
½ CUP CURRANTS, RINSED IN WARM WATER	125 mL
2 TBSP. BROWN SUGAR	30 mL
1½ TSP. CUMIN	7 mL
1 TSP. GRATED ORANGE RIND	5 mL
2 BAY LEAVES	
3" CINNAMON STICK	7 cm
½ CUP CHOPPED FRESH PARSLEY	125 mL
1-2 TSP. SALT	5-10 mL
1 TSP. FRESHLY GROUND PEPPER	5 mL

TRIM LAMB AND CUT INTO BITE-SIZED PIECES. IN DUTCH OVEN, BROWN LAMB IN 3 BATCHES USING 1 TBSP. OIL WITH EACH BATCH. RETURN LAMB (AND ALL THOSE ACCUMULATED JUICES) TO THE POT. ADD ONIONS AND GARLIC AND COOK COVERED UNTIL ONIONS ARE SOFTENED. PURÉE TOMATOES AND ADD TO POT. ADD REMAINING INGREDIENTS AND BRING TO BOIL. REDUCE HEAT AND SIMMER COVERED AT LEAST 1 HOUR. DISCARD BAY LEAVES AND CINNAMON STICK. SERVES 8.

THE FLAVOR IMPROVES IF YOU MAKE THIS DELICIOUS STEW THE DAY BEFORE - THAT WAY, YOU CAN MAKE APPLE PECAN PHYLLO CRISPS (PAGE 190) FOR DESSERT THE DAY YOU'RE EXPECTING COMPANY.

PORK TENDERLOIN WITH HONEY-GLAZED APPLES

MARINADE

1/3 CUP APPLE JUICE	75 mL
1/4 CUP HONEY, MELTED	60 mL
2 TBSP. SOY SAUCE	30 mL
2 TBSP. VEGETABLE OIL	30 mL
1 TSP. DIJON MUSTARD	5 mL
4 GREEN ONIONS, CHOPPED	
2 CLOVES GARLIC, MINCED	
1 TBSP. GRATED FRESH GINGER	15 mL
2 LBS. PORK TENDERLOIN	1 kg

GLAZED APPLES

1 TBSP. BUTTER	15 mL
1 TBSP. HONEY	15 mL
1 TBSP. LEMON JUICE	15 mL
2 APPLES, PEELED AND THINLY SLICED	

PUT MARINADE INGREDIENTS INTO A LARGE SEALABLE PLASTIC BAG AND MIX. ADD PORK. SEAL AND REFRIGERATE OVERNIGHT OR AT LEAST 4 HOURS. REMOVE PORK AND PLACE IN SHALLOW DISH. POUR MARINADE OVER. BAKE AT 350°F FOR 40-50 MINUTES. COVER AND LET STAND 10 MINUTES.

TO GLAZE APPLES: IN FRYING PAN HEAT BUTTER, HONEY AND LEMON JUICE TOGETHER. ADD APPLES AND TOSS TO COAT. COOK 2 OR 3 MINUTES. SLICE PORK AND SPOON GLAZED APPLES OVER TOP. ENJOY! SERVES 4.

ROAST PORK LOIN WITH APPLE TOPPING

½ TSP. SUGAR	2 mL
2 TBSP. FLOUR	30 mL
1½ TSP. SALT	7 mL
1 TSP. DRY MUSTARD	5 mL
1 TSP. CARAWAY SEEDS	5 mL
¼ TSP. BLACK PEPPER	1 mL
¼ TSP. GROUND SAGE	1 mL
4-5 LB. PORK LOIN ROAST	2-2.2 kg

TOPPING

1½ CUPS APPLESAUCE (OR MINCED APPLE)	375 mL
½ CUP BROWN SUGAR	125 mL
¼ TSP. CINNAMON	1 mL
¼ TSP. MACE	1 mL
¼ TSP. SALT	1 mL
SMALL AMOUNT OF WATER FOR GRAVY	

MIX SUGAR, FLOUR, SALT, MUSTARD, CARAWAY SEEDS, PEPPER AND SAGE TOGETHER. RUB MIXTURE OVER SURFACE OF PORK. PLACE FAT SIDE UP IN ROASTING PAN AND BAKE AT 325°F FOR 1½ HOURS. MIX TOPPING INGREDIENTS AND SPREAD OVER ROAST. BAKE 1 HOUR LONGER, ADD WATER TO BOTTOM OF PAN TO MAKE EXCELLENT GRAVY. DON'T FORGET THE APPLESAUCE.

THE MORE A WOMAN HAS TO BE ON HER TOES, THE LESS YOU WILL SEE HER IN 4-INCH HEELS.

STUFFED PORK TENDERLOIN

2 LBS. PORK TENDERLOIN	1 kg

MARINADE

2 TBSP. VEGETABLE OIL	30 mL
2 TBSP. SOY SAUCE	30 mL
2 TBSP. LEMON JUICE	30 mL

STUFFING

3 TBSP. BUTTER	45 mL
2 STALKS CELERY, FINELY CHOPPED	
½ CUP FINELY CHOPPED ONION	125 mL
1 CUP CHOPPED MUSHROOMS	250 mL
1 CUP BREADCRUMBS	250 mL
2 TSP. ROSEMARY	10 mL
2 TSP. BASIL	10 mL
2 TBSP. MADEIRA (USE PORT OR SHERRY AS AN ALTERNATIVE)	30 mL

BUTTERFLY TENDERLOIN (PARTIALLY CUT LENGTH-WISE TO FLATTEN). MARINATE FOR SEVERAL HOURS. SAUTÉ CELERY, ONION AND MUSHROOMS IN BUTTER UNTIL SOFT. ADD REMAINING INGREDIENTS AND BLENDERIZE TO FORM FINE MIXTURE. SPREAD STUFFING DOWN CENTER OF TENDERLOIN. FOLD OVER AND TIE OR SKEWER SECURELY. BAKE AT 350°F FOR 40 MINUTES. CUT IN THICK SLICES AND SERVE WITH RICE, APPLESAUCE AND VEGGIES.

HUMAN BEINGS ARE THE ONLY CREATURES THAT ALLOW THEIR CHILDREN TO COME BACK HOME.

CAJUN PORK CUTLETS

¼ TSP. BLACK PEPPER	1 mL
¼ TSP. PAPRIKA	1 mL
¼ TSP. CAYENNE	1 mL
¼ TSP. OREGANO	1 mL
¼ TSP. THYME	1 mL
¼ TSP. GINGER	1 mL
4 PORK CUTLETS	
2 TBSP. BUTTER	30 mL
SALT TO TASTE	
1 ONION, SLICED	
1 GREEN PEPPER, SLICED IN STRIPS	
1 RED PEPPER, SLICED IN STRIPS	
2 TBSP. FLOUR	30 mL
1½ CUPS CHICKEN STOCK, HEATED	375 mL
1 TSP. HONEY	5 mL

MIX SPICES. RUB HALF OF THE MIXTURE INTO CUTLETS. HEAT BUTTER IN LARGE FRYING PAN OVER MEDIUM HEAT. ADD PORK AND COOK 3 MINUTES PER SIDE. SEASON WITH SALT AND SET ASIDE. ADD ONION TO HOT PAN AND COOK 3 MINUTES OVER MEDIUM HEAT. ADD PEPPERS AND REMAINING SPICE MIXTURE. MIX AND COOK 7 MINUTES. SPRINKLE IN FLOUR, MIX WELL AND COOK 3 MINUTES. SLOWLY ADD CHICKEN STOCK AND HONEY. COOK 5 MINUTES OVER LOW HEAT. RETURN PORK TO PAN AND SIMMER ANOTHER 2 MINUTES. SERVE WITH RICE AND BROCCOLI. SERVES 4.

THE SHORTEST DISTANCE BETWEEN TWO POINTS IS USUALLY UNDER REPAIR.

THESE WILL FILL UP EVERY COOKIE JAR YOU OWN — THEY FREEZE WELL!

1 CUP BUTTER	250 mL
1 CUP SUGAR	250 mL
1 CUP BROWN SUGAR	250 mL
1 EGG	
1 CUP VEGETABLE OIL	250 mL
1 TSP. VANILLA	5 mL
1 CUP ROLLED OATS	250 mL
1 CUP CRUSHED CORNFLAKES	250 mL
½ CUP SHREDDED COCONUT	125 mL
½ CUP CHOPPED WALNUTS OR PECANS	125 mL
3½ CUPS FLOUR	875 mL
1 TSP. BAKING SODA	5 mL
1 TSP. SALT	5 mL

PREHEAT OVEN TO 325°F. CREAM TOGETHER BUTTER AND SUGARS UNTIL LIGHT AND FLUFFY. ADD EGG, OIL AND VANILLA. MIX WELL. ADD OATS, CORNFLAKES, COCONUT AND NUTS. STIR WELL. ADD FLOUR, SODA AND SALT. STIR UNTIL WELL BLENDED. DROP BY TEASPOONFULS ON GREASED COOKIE SHEETS AND FLATTEN WITH FORK DIPPED IN WATER. BAKE 15 MINUTES. MAKES 8 DOZEN.

MEN DON'T CARE WHAT'S ON TV. THEY ONLY CARE WHAT ELSE IS ON TV.

DATE-FILLED COOKIES

Here's another old favorite you need for your cookie jar.

DATE FILLING

2 CUPS FINELY CHOPPED DATES	500 mL
1 CUP WATER	250 mL
1 TBSP. SUGAR	15 mL
2 TBSP. LEMON JUICE	30 mL

COOKIE DOUGH

2 CUPS FLOUR	500 mL
1½ TSP. BAKING SODA	7 mL
1 TSP. SALT	5 mL
2 CUPS BROWN SUGAR	500 mL
6 CUPS ROLLED OATS	1.5 L
1 CUP VEGETABLE OIL	250 mL
⅞ CUP COLD WATER	220 mL

TO MAKE FILLING: COMBINE ALL INGREDIENTS IN A SAUCEPAN AND COOK OVER MEDIUM HEAT UNTIL THE DATES ARE SOFT AND MIXTURE IS SPREADABLE. STIR CONSTANTLY. REMOVE FROM HEAT AND COOL.

TO MAKE COOKIES: PREHEAT OVEN TO 350°F. MIX TOGETHER FLOUR, BAKING SODA AND SALT. ADD BROWN SUGAR, OATS AND OIL. COMBINE WELL WITH FORK, SPRINKLING WITH WATER AND MIXING TO MAKE SOFT BUT NOT STICKY DOUGH. ROLL DOUGH VERY THIN. CUT OUT 2" CIRCLES WITH FLOURED COOKIE CUTTER. BAKE 5-7 MINUTES AND COOL. SPREAD COOLED DATE FILLING ON HALF OF THE COOKIES AND PLACE OTHER COOKIE HALVES ON TOP TO FORM SANDWICHES. MAKES ABOUT 6 DOZEN. (PICTURED ON PAGE 71.)

ONE CUP OF EVERYTHING COOKIES

MOIST AND CHEWY - GOOD KID'S STUFF!

1 CUP MARGARINE	250 mL
1 CUP BROWN SUGAR	250 mL
1 CUP WHITE SUGAR	250 mL
3 EGGS	
1 CUP PEANUT BUTTER	250 mL
1 CUP COCONUT	250 mL
1 CUP CHOCOLATE CHIPS	250 mL
1 CUP FLOUR	250 mL
1 TBSP. BAKING SODA (SO WE LIED!)	15 mL
1 CUP OATMEAL	250 mL
1 CUP RAISINS	250 mL
1 CUP PECANS, CHOPPED	250 mL

PREHEAT OVEN TO 350°F. BEAT MARGARINE, BOTH SUGARS, EGGS AND PEANUT BUTTER UNTIL CREAMY. ADD REMAINING INGREDIENTS AND MIX WELL. DROP BY SPOONFULS ON COOKIE SHEET AND BAKE FOR 10 MINUTES. MAKES 9 DOZEN.

THE BEST THING ABOUT CHILDREN'S BIRTHDAY PARTIES IS THAT THEY PROVE THERE ARE CHILDREN WHO BEHAVE WORSE THAN YOUR OWN.

SKOR BAR COOKIES

CHEWY TREATS FOR YOUR FAVORITE PEOPLE.

1 CUP MARGARINE OR BUTTER	250 mL
3/4 BROWN SUGAR	175 mL
1/2 CUP SUGAR	125 mL
1 EGG	
2 TBSP. MILK	30 mL
2 TSP. VANILLA	10 mL
1 3/4 CUPS FLOUR	425 mL
3/4 CUP ROLLED OATS	175 mL
1 TSP. BAKING SODA	5 mL
1/4 TSP. SALT	1 mL
4 SKOR BARS OR ANY CRUNCHY TOFFEE CHOCOLATE-COATED BARS, BROKEN INTO SMALL PIECES	4 - 39 g
1 CUP SLIVERED ALMONDS, TOASTED	250 mL

PREHEAT OVEN TO 350°F. CREAM MARGARINE, SUGARS, EGG, MILK AND VANILLA IN LARGE BOWL. BEAT UNTIL LIGHT AND CREAMY. COMBINE FLOUR, OATS, BAKING SODA AND SALT. ADD TO CREAMED MIXTURE AND BLEND WELL. STIR IN TOFFEE BAR PIECES AND ALMONDS. DROP DOUGH BY TEASPOONFULS ON GREASED COOKIE SHEET. (LEAVE ROOM FOR SPREADING - THE COOKIES, NOT YOU!) BAKE 8-10 MINUTES, OR UNTIL GOLDEN. COOL SLIGHTLY, THEN REMOVE TO COOLING RACK. (PICTURED ON PAGE 71.)

LEAKPROOF SEALS - WILL.

CHOCOLATE ESPRESSO COOKIES

SPECIAL ENOUGH TO SERVE AT A DINNER PARTY WITH A DISH OF FRESH STRAWBERRIES.

1 CUP FLOUR	250 mL
½ CUP COCOA	125 mL
½ TSP. SALT	2 mL
¼ TSP. BAKING SODA	1 mL
3 TBSP. UNSALTED BUTTER	45 mL
3 TBSP. MARGARINE	45 mL
½ CUP PLUS 2 TBSP. SUGAR	155 mL
½ CUP BROWN SUGAR	125 mL
1 ½ TBSP. INSTANT ESPRESSO POWDER OR INSTANT COFFEE POWDER	22 mL
1 TSP. VANILLA	5 mL
1 EGG WHITE	

SIFT FLOUR, COCOA, SALT AND BAKING SODA IN A SMALL BOWL. BEAT BUTTER AND MARGARINE UNTIL CREAMY. ADD SUGARS, ESPRESSO POWDER AND VANILLA AND BEAT UNTIL BLENDED. MIX IN EGG WHITE. ADD DRY INGREDIENTS AND BEAT JUST UNTIL BLENDED. KNEAD UNTIL DOUGH IS SMOOTH. WRAP DOUGH IN WAX PAPER AND REFRIGERATE FOR 1 HOUR. PREHEAT OVEN TO 350°F. ROLL OUT DOUGH TO ¼" THICKNESS ON BOARD SPRINKLED WITH ICING SUGAR AND CUT IN 2" CIRCLES. BAKE 10-12 MINUTES. MAKES 3-4 DOZEN CRISP COOKIES. (PICTURED ON PAGE 71.)

 2 GRAMS FAT PER COOKIE

ABOUT THE ONLY THING YOU CAN DO ON A SHOESTRING IS TRIP.

THESE ARE EASIER TO MAKE THAN THEY ARE TO SAY!

3/4 CUP UNSALTED BUTTER, ROOM TEMPERATURE	175 mL
1/2 CUP SUGAR	125 mL
2 EGG YOLKS	
1 TSP. VANILLA	5 mL
2 CUPS FLOUR	500 mL
VANILLA SUGAR TO SPRINKLE	
2-OZ. SEMISWEET CHOCOLATE	60 g

BEAT BUTTER AND SUGAR UNTIL LIGHT. BEAT IN YOLKS AND VANILLA. GRADUALLY BEAT IN FLOUR AND TURN DOUGH ONTO A COUNTER. KNEAD UNTIL WELL COMBINED. FORM INTO A BALL. COVER WITH A BOWL AND LET STAND FOR 2 HOURS. PREHEAT OVEN TO 375°F. TO MAKE EACH COOKIE, SHAPE 1 TBSP. OF DOUGH INTO A CRESCENT. PLACE COOKIES ON UNGREASED COOKIE SHEET AND BAKE 10-12 MINUTES (COOKIES WILL BE WHITE). SPRINKLE WITH VANILLA SUGAR AND COOL COMPLETELY. MELT CHOCOLATE IN TOP OF DOUBLE BOILER OR MICROWAVE. DIP TIPS OF EACH COOKIE IN CHOCOLATE AND PLACE ON WAX PAPER TO SET. MAKES 2-2 1/2 DOZEN VERY PROFESSIONAL LOOKING COOKIES - KATINKA SAYS ENJOY! (PICTURED ON PAGE 71.)

IF I DIE, I FORGIVE YOU; IF I LIVE, WE'LL SEE.

A CRISP AND EASY REFRIGERATOR COOKIE - SERVE WITH MARGUARITA FRUIT COCKTAIL (PAGE 207).

½ CUP BUTTER	125 mL
1 CUP SUGAR	250 mL
1 EGG	
1 TBSP. GRATED LEMON RIND	15 mL
2 TBSP. LEMON JUICE	30 mL
2 CUPS FLOUR	500 mL
½ TSP. SALT	2 mL
½ TSP. BAKING SODA	2 mL
½ TSP. GINGER	2 mL
SUGAR TO SPRINKLE	

CREAM TOGETHER BUTTER AND SUGAR. BEAT IN EGG, LEMON RIND AND JUICE. COMBINE FLOUR, SALT, BAKING SODA, AND GINGER AND GRADUALLY BLEND INTO CREAMED MIXTURE. SHAPE INTO 2 LOGS 1¾" IN DIAMETER. WRAP IN WAXED PAPER AND REFRIGERATE FOR 3 HOURS. PREHEAT OVEN TO 375°F. CUT INTO ⅛" THICK SLICES. PLACE ON GREASED COOKIE SHEET ABOUT 2" APART AND SPRINKLE WITH SUGAR. BAKE 6-8 MINUTES, UNTIL LIGHTLY BROWNED AROUND THE EDGES. COOL BEFORE REMOVING FROM PAN. STORE IN LOOSELY SEALED CONTAINER TO MAINTAIN CRISPNESS. (PICTURED ON PAGE 71.)

DOES THE NAME PAVLOV RING A BELL?

BROWN SUGAR SHORTBREAD

THIS RECIPE COMES FROM THE OTHER SIDE OF THE FAMILY.

1 LB. BUTTER	500 g
1 CUP GOLDEN BROWN SUGAR	250 mL
4½ CUPS FLOUR	1.125 L
PINCH OF SALT	
PINCH OF BAKING SODA	

CREAM BUTTER UNTIL VERY SOFT. ADD SUGAR AND MIX WELL. ADD FLOUR 1 CUP AT A TIME, BEATING WELL EACH TIME. ROLL ¼" THICK AND CUT IN SHAPES WITH COOKIE CUTTER. BAKE AT 350°F FOR 10 MINUTES.

HOW DID A FOOL AND HIS MONEY EVER GET TOGETHER ANYWAY?

TIGER BUTTER

1 LB. GOOD QUALITY WHITE CHOCOLATE	500 g
¾ CUP PEANUT BUTTER	175 mL
2 OZ. GOOD QUALITY DARK CHOCOLATE	55 g

MELT WHITE CHOCOLATE AND PEANUT BUTTER IN MICROWAVE OR DOUBLE BOILER UNTIL SMOOTH. (DON'T LET IT SCORCH!) POUR ONTO COOKIE SHEET LINED WITH WAXED PAPER. MELT DARK CHOCOLATE AND DRIZZLE OVER PEANUT BUTTER MIXTURE. SWIRL WITH A KNIFE. REFRIGERATE TO SET. CUT OR BREAK INTO PIECES.

TURTLES

THESE ARE BETTER THAN STORE BOUGHT!

50 CARAMELS, UNWRAPPED
2 TBSP. HALF & HALF CREAM   30 mL
1½ LBS. GOOD-QUALITY MILK CHOCOLATE   750 mL
150 WHOLE PECANS

PLACE CARAMELS IN FREEZER FOR ½ HOUR - WRAPPERS COME OFF IN A FLASH! MELT CARAMELS OVER LOW HEAT AND ADD CREAM. IN A DOUBLE BOILER, MELT CHOCOLATE TO A SMOOTH CONSISTENCY. LINE A COOKIE SHEET WITH WAXED PAPER. TO MAKE EACH TURTLE, PLACE 3 PECANS ON THE COOKIE SHEET, IN A "Y" SHAPE OR IF THE PECANS ARE LARGE, 2 ON THE BOTTOM AND 1 SITTING ON TOP. TURTLES SHOULD BE 1"-2" APART. SPOON 1 TSP. OF CARAMEL MIXTURE OVER THE TOP OF THE PECANS. PLACE IN FREEZER FOR 15 MINUTES. PICK UP A TURTLE WITH A FORK AND SUBMERGE IN MELTED CHOCOLATE. HOLD ABOVE PAN UNTIL IT STOPS DRIPPING AND REPLACE ON THE WAXED PAPER LINED COOKIE SHEET. LET TURTLES SET IN REFRIGERATOR. STORE IN AN AIRTIGHT CONTAINER AND KEEP IN A COOL PLACE.
MAKES 50 TURTLES.

ENGAGEMENT: A PERIOD OF URGE ON THE VERGE OF A MERGE.

XMAS TOFFEE

YOUR KIDS WILL LOVE HELPING YOU --- FOR THE FIRST 3 MINUTES! SOFT CHEWY CANDIES.

1 LB. BUTTER	500 g
4 CUPS WHITE SUGAR	1 L
10-OZ. CAN SWEETENED CONDENSED MILK	300 mL
16-OZ. BOTTLE GOLDEN CORN SYRUP	500 mL

MIX ALL INGREDIENTS IN LARGE SAUCEPAN. GRADUALLY BRING TO BOIL. COOK 20-30 MINUTES, STIRRING CONSTANTLY, TO SOFT BALL STAGE. (USE CANDY THERMOMETER.) POUR ONTO 2 WELL-BUTTERED COOKIE SHEETS. WHEN SET CUT INTO SMALL PIECES AND WRAP IN WAXED PAPER - TWISTING BOTH ENDS CLOSED. MAKES 20 DOZEN.

CHEWY TOFFEE CANDY

NOW YOU CAN MAKE ONE OF GRANDMA'S TREATS.

6 - 2-OZ. MACINTOSH TOFFEE BARS	6 - 56 g
4 TBSP. CREAM	60 mL
2 TBSP. BUTTER	30 mL
4 CUPS CORNFLAKES	1 L
1 CUP COARSELY CHOPPED PECANS	250 mL

MELT TOFFEE IN DOUBLE BOILER. BEAT IN CREAM AND BUTTER. ADD CORNFLAKES AND PECANS. BUTTER HANDS AND SHAPE TOFFEE IN LITTLE BALLS ON WAXED PAPER. COOL AND CONSUME! CAN BE INDIVIDUALLY WRAPPED IN PLASTIC WRAP.

NUTCHOS

CALL THEM COOKIES - CALL THEM CANDIES -
CALL THEM DELICIOUS!

2 - 10-OZ. PKGS. SEMISWEET CHOCOLATE CHIPS	2 - 300 g
10-OZ. PKG. PEANUT BUTTER CHIPS	300 g
2 CUPS SALTED PEANUTS	500 mL
7-OZ. BOX RIPPLE POTATO CHIPS, COARSELY CRUMBLED	200 g

IN A DOUBLE BOILER, MELT CHOCOLATE AND
PEANUT BUTTER CHIPS. STIR IN PEANUTS AND
CRUMBLED CHIPS. DROP ON WAXED PAPER AND
LEAVE TO COOL. STORE IN THE REFRIGERATOR. YOU
CAN ALSO FREEZE THESE AND EAT THEM WHEN
YOU'RE DOING THE LAUNDRY! MAKES ABOUT 48.

YOU CAN ALWAYS TELL A TEXAN, BUT NOT TOO MUCH!

E-Z POPCORN BALLS

ANOTHER BONDING EXPERIENCE! - WHERE IS
JAMES!

1 CUP SUGAR	250 mL
1/3 CUP MARGARINE	75 mL
1/2 CUP CORN SYRUP	125 mL
2 TSP. VANILLA	10 mL
18 CUPS POPPED POPCORN	4.5 L

BOIL SUGAR, MARGARINE, CORN SYRUP AND
VANILLA FOR 3 MINUTES. POUR OVER POPCORN AND
FORM BALLS WHILE STILL WARM. COOL AND WRAP

CRISPIX MIX

12-oz. BOX CRISPIX CEREAL	350 g
3 CUPS WHOLE PECANS	750 mL
3 CUPS WHOLE ALMONDS	750 mL
½ CUP BUTTER OR MARGARINE	125 mL
2 CUPS BROWN SUGAR	500 mL
1 CUP CORN SYRUP	250 mL
1½ TSP. VANILLA	7 mL

PREHEAT OVEN TO 250°F. MIX CRISPIX, PECANS AND ALMONDS TOGETHER IN A LARGE ROASTER. SET ASIDE. IN SAUCEPAN MIX BUTTER, BROWN SUGAR AND CORN SYRUP. BOIL UNTIL SOFT BALL STAGE (A CANDY THERMOMETER IS A GOOD IDEA.) REMOVE FROM HEAT AND ADD VANILLA. POUR OVER CRISPIX, MIX AND STIR THROUGHLY. PLACE IN OVEN FOR 1 HOUR, STIRRING EVERY 15 MINUTES. REMOVE FROM OVEN AND GIVE IT A STIR EVERYTIME YOU WALK PAST. AFTER AN HOUR, PACK WHAT YOU HAVEN'T ALREADY EATEN AND PRESENT TO FRIENDS, HOSTESSES AND BEAVER LEADERS.

THE EXERCISE THAT REALLY CHANGES YOUR LIFE IS WALKING DOWN THE AISLE.

REMEMBER THIS OLD FAVORITE WITH THE PRIZE IN THE BOX? NOW YOU'VE GOT THE RECIPE.

24 CUPS POPPED CORN (1 CUP UNPOPPED)	6 L
1 CUP MARGARINE OR BUTTER	250 mL
2 CUPS BROWN SUGAR	500 mL
1/2 CUP CORN SYRUP	125 mL
1 TSP. SALT	5 mL
1/2 TSP. BAKING SODA	2 mL
1 TSP. VANILLA	5 mL
1 CUP PEANUTS	250 mL

PREHEAT OVEN TO 250°F. PUT POPCORN IN LARGE BOWL. MELT MARGARINE, STIR IN BROWN SUGAR, CORN SYRUP AND SALT. BRING TO BOIL, STIRRING CONSTANTLY. BOIL FOR 5 MINUTES WITHOUT STIRRING. REMOVE FROM HEAT, STIR IN BAKING SODA AND VANILLA, THEN PEANUTS. POUR OVER POPPED CORN AND MIX WELL. PUT IN LARGE ROASTING PAN AND BAKE FOR 1 HOUR, STIRRING EVERY 15 MINUTES. REMOVE FROM OVEN, COOL AND BREAK INTO PIECES. STORE IN TIGHTLY COVERED TIN BOX. (IF THE KIDS DON'T FIND IT FIRST!) MAKES 6 QUARTS.

ALL MEN MAKE MISTAKES, BUT MARRIED MEN FIND OUT ABOUT THEM SOONER.

CHOCOLATE CRUNCH BARS

THESE NO-BAKE BARS ARE EASY FOR KIDS TO MAKE.

1 CUP PEANUT BUTTER	250 mL
1 CUP PACKED BROWN SUGAR	250 mL
½ CUP CORN SYRUP	125 mL
½ CUP LIQUID HONEY	125 mL
1 CUP CHOPPED PEANUTS	250 mL
1 TSP. VANILLA	5 mL
8 CUPS CORNFLAKES	2 L
2 CUPS CHOCOLATE CHIPS	500 mL
2 TBSP. MARGARINE	30 mL

IN LARGE SAUCEPAN, COMBINE PEANUT BUTTER, BROWN SUGAR, CORN SYRUP AND HONEY; STIR OVER MEDIUM HEAT UNTIL SMOOTH. REMOVE FROM HEAT AND STIR IN PEANUTS AND VANILLA. GRADUALLY ADD CEREAL, STIRRING UNTIL WELL COATED. PRESS EVENLY INTO A GREASED 15" X 10" JELLY-ROLL PAN. IN DOUBLE BOILER MELT CHOCOLATE AND MARGARINE. SPREAD EVENLY OVER MIXTURE IN PAN. CHILL UNTIL SET. CUT INTO BARS. MAKES ABOUT 50.

SHOW ME A WOMAN THAT DOESN'T FEEL GUILTY AND I'LL SHOW YOU A MAN.

TOFFEE KRISPS

HOORAY - RICE KRISPIE SQUARES FOR THE '90S!

2 - 2-OZ. MACINTOSH TOFFEE BARS, BROKEN	2 - 56 g
2 TBSP. CREAM	30 mL
2½ CUPS RICE KRISPIES	625 mL

MELT TOFFEE PIECES WITH CREAM IN DOUBLE BOILER, STIRRING CONSTANTLY UNTIL MIXTURE IS WELL BLENDED. ADD RICE KRISPIES AND MIX UNTIL COATED. PRESS INTO GREASED 8" x 8" PAN. COOL AND CUT INTO SQUARES.

THE BEST WAY TO STAND ON YOUR OWN TWO FEET IS TO STOP MAKING PAYMENTS ON YOUR CAR.

GOOD OLD RICE KRISPIE SQUARES

NOW THIS OLD FAVORITE IS SOMEPLACE WHERE YOU CAN FIND IT!

¼ CUP MARGARINE	60 mL
8-OZ. PKG. MINIATURE MARSHMALLOWS OR 40 REGULAR-SIZE MARSHMALLOWS (BUY GOOD QUALITY OR THEY WON'T MELT PROPERLY!)	250 g
½ TSP. VANILLA	2 mL
6 CUPS RICE KRISPIES	1.5 L

MELT MARGARINE, ADD MARSHMALLOWS AND STIR UNTIL MELTED. ADD VANILLA AND RICE KRISPIES AND MIX UNTIL ALL ARE COATED. PRESS INTO GREASED 9" x 13" PAN. COOL AND CUT INTO SQUARES.

THE UNTURTLE BAR

A "MUST MAKE" FOR THE HOLIDAYS.

2 CUPS FLOUR	500 mL
I CUP PACKED BROWN SUGAR	250 mL
½ CUP MARGARINE, SOFTENED	125 mL
I CUP PECAN HALVES	250 mL
⅔ CUP MARGARINE	150 mL
½ CUP PACKED BROWN SUGAR	125 mL
I CUP SEMISWEET CHOCOLATE CHIPS	250 mL

PREHEAT OVEN TO 350°F. BEAT TOGETHER FLOUR, SUGAR AND ½ CUP MARGARINE. PRESS FIRMLY INTO UNGREASED 9" X 13" PAN. ARRANGE PECANS OVER CRUST. COMBINE MARGARINE AND BROWN SUGAR IN SAUCEPAN AND BRING TO BOIL, STIRRING CONSTANTLY FOR I MINUTE. POUR OVER PECANS. BAKE 15-20 MINUTES, OR UNTIL BUBBLY. SPRINKLE CHOCOLATE CHIPS OVER TOP, LET STAND FOR 3 MINUTES AND SPREAD CHOCOLATE. COOL COMPLETELY AND CUT INTO SMALL SQUARES. YUM! YUM! MAKES 40.

WHEN ALL THE CHILDREN HAVE GROWN UP AND MOVED AWAY, MOST PARENTS EXPERIENCE A STRANGE NEW EMOTION - ECSTASY.

JOSHUA'S MOM'S SKATING BARS

TAKE THIS TO YOUR NEXT FUNCTION - JOSHUA'S MOM DID! MOIST AND CHEWY.

½ CUP FLOUR	125 mL
¼ CUP BROWN SUGAR	60 mL
¼ TSP. BAKING POWDER	1 mL
PINCH OF SALT	
¾ CUP ROLLED OATS	175 mL
⅓ CUP COLD BUTTER	75 mL
2 EGGS	
¾ CUP PACKED BROWN SUGAR	175 mL
1 TBSP. ORANGE JUICE	15 mL
GRATED RIND OF 1 ORANGE	
¾ CUP FLAKED COCONUT	175 mL
¾ CUP RAISINS	175 mL

PREHEAT OVEN TO 350°F. COMBINE FLOUR, BROWN SUGAR, BAKING POWDER, SALT AND ROLLED OATS. CUT IN BUTTER UNTIL CRUMBLY AND PRESS INTO A LIGHTLY GREASED 8" SQUARE PAN. BAKE FOR 15 MINUTES, OR UNTIL GOLDEN. IN THE SAME BOWL, BEAT EGGS WITH BROWN SUGAR, ORANGE JUICE AND RIND. STIR IN COCONUT AND RAISINS. POUR OVER BAKED CRUST AND RETURN TO OVEN FOR 20-25 MINUTES, OR UNTIL GOLDEN. COOL BEFORE CUTTING. MAKES 16-20 BARS.

DON'T FRY BACON WITH YOUR SHIRT OFF.

THIS TASTES JUST LIKE AN EAT-MORE BAR. GREAT IN BACK PACK AND LUNCH BOXES TOO! MAKE SURE YOU HAVE ALL THE INGREDIENTS MEASURED AND READY TO ADD TO THE POT.

3/4 CUP HONEY	175 mL
1 CUP PEANUT BUTTER	250 mL
10 REGULAR-SIZE MARSHMALLOWS	
1 CUP CHOCOLATE CHIPS	250 mL
1 CUP PEANUTS	250 mL
3 CUPS RICE KRISPIES	750 mL

IN A LARGE POT BRING HONEY AND PEANUT BUTTER TO A BOIL OVER MEDIUM HEAT. STIR CONSTANTLY. ADD MARSHMALLOWS AND CHOCOLATE CHIPS, STIRRING UNTIL MELTED. REMOVE FROM HEAT AND STIR IN PEANUTS AND RICE KRISPIES. PRESS INTO A 9" X 13" PAN. COOL AND BE READY TO EAT... MORE!

SIGN IN TRAVEL AGENCY WINDOW: "BOOK YOUR FLIGHT WITH US AND WE'LL SEND YOUR LUGGAGE ALL OVER THE WORLD."

CARAMEL NUT BROWNIES

THESE ARE AMAZING - YOU WON'T BELIEVE THERE'S A CAKE MIX IN THIS RECIPE, BUT YOU WILL KNOW ABOUT THE CARAMELS BY THE TIME YOU UNWRAP 50 OF THE LITTLE SUCKERS!

50 CARAMELS, UNWRAPPED!! - YUP!	
2/3 CUP EVAPORATED MILK, DIVIDED	150 mL
19-OZ. GERMAN CHOCOLATE CAKE MIX	520 g
(DEVIL'S FOOD WILL DO)	
3/4 CUP BUTTER, MELTED	175 mL
1 CUP CHOCOLATE CHIPS	250 mL
1 CUP PECANS, CHOPPED	250 mL

PREHEAT OVEN TO 350°F. MELT CARAMELS WITH 1/3 CUP EVAPORATED MILK, STIRRING FREQUENTLY. COMBINE CAKE MIX, MELTED BUTTER AND REMAINING 1/3 CUP EVAPORATED MILK. SPREAD HALF OF THIS MIXTURE INTO A GREASED 9" X 13" PAN. BAKE FOR 6-8 MINUTES. REMOVE PAN FROM OVEN AND SPRINKLE WITH CHOCOLATE CHIPS AND PECANS. DRIZZLE WITH MELTED CARAMELS AND COVER WITH REMAINING CAKE BATTER. RETURN TO OVEN AND BAKE FOR 15 MINUTES. COOL BEFORE SLICING. CUT IN SMALL PIECES - IT'S JUST LIKE FUDGE.

CHRISTMAS COMMENT: JUST SEND THE FIVE GOLD RINGS AND CANCEL THE REST OF MY TRUE LOVE'S ORDER.

APPLE BROWNIES

THIS IS IT - EVERYONE'S NEXT FAVORITE.

1 CUP MARGARINE	250 mL
½ TSP. SALT	2 mL
2 CUPS SUGAR	500 mL
2 EGGS, BEATEN	
2 CUPS FLOUR	500 mL
1 TSP. BAKING POWDER	5 mL
1 TSP. BAKING SODA	5 mL
1 TSP. CINNAMON	5 mL
2 CUPS PEELED, SLICED GRANNY SMITH APPLES	500 mL
½ CUP CHOPPED PECANS OR WALNUTS	125 mL

PREHEAT OVEN TO 325°F. GREASE A 9" X 13" PAN. CREAM TOGETHER MARGARINE, SALT AND SUGAR. BEAT IN EGGS AND MIX WELL. ADD DRY INGREDIENTS AND MIX WELL. ADD APPLE SLICES AND NUTS. MIXTURE IS QUITE THICK - DON'T BE SNITCHING ANY DOUGH! SPREAD EVENLY IN PAN AND BAKE FOR 35-40 MINUTES. SERVE WARM WITH VANILLA ICE CREAM.

I HAD MY CAT NEUTERED. HE'S STILL OUT ALL NIGHT WITH THE OTHER CATS, BUT NOW IT'S ONLY AS A CONSULTANT.

A LIGHTER VERSION OF THE TRADITIONAL MINCEMEAT TART.

8 SHEETS PHYLLO PASTRY, THAWED	
COOKING SPRAY	
8 OZ. LIGHT CREAM CHEESE, SOFTENED	250 g
½ CUP ICING SUGAR	125 mL
2 TSP. LIME JUICE	10 mL
1 CUP MINCEMEAT	250 mL
¼ CUP SLIVERED ALMONDS, TOASTED	60 mL

PLACE 1 SHEET OF PHYLLO ON FLAT SURFACE AND LIGHTLY SPRAY WITH COOKING SPRAY. TOP WITH SECOND PHYLLO SHEET, SPRAY AND REPEAT WITH 2 MORE SHEETS. CUT STACKED PHYLLO LENGTHWISE INTO 4 STRIPS; CUT EACH STRIP CROSSWISE INTO 5 PIECES SO THAT YOU HAVE 20 STACKS. PRESS EACH STACK OF PHYLLO INTO EACH OF 20 MINI MUFFIN CUPS TO MAKE TINY TART SHELLS. PREHEAT OVEN TO 350°F. BAKE 10-12 MINUTES, UNTIL GOLDEN BROWN. REMOVE PAN TO WIRE RACK TO COOL SLIGHTLY. REMOVE TART SHELLS FROM MUFFIN PAN; COOL. REPEAT WITH REMAINING PHYLLO TO MAKE 20 MORE TART SHELLS.

IN SMALL BOWL, BEAT CREAM CHEESE, ICING SUGAR AND LIME JUICE ON LOW SPEED UNTIL BLENDED. REFRIGERATE UNTIL SERVING TIME.

TO SERVE, SPOON 1 ROUNDED TEASPOON MINCEMEAT INTO EACH TART SHELL AND SPOON

MINCEMEAT TARTS

THIS RECIPE CONTINUED FROM PAGE 184.

CREAM CHEESE MIXTURE ON TOP OF EACH TART. SPRINKLE WITH TOASTED ALMONDS. MAKES 40 TARTS.

☼ LESS THAN 3 GRAMS FAT IN EACH TINY LITTLE TART!

LEMON SAUCE

EXCELLENT FOR CAKES AND GINGERBREAD

1 LEMON, JUICE AND GRATED RIND	
1¼ CUPS BOILING WATER	300 mL
2 TBSP. CORNSTARCH	30 mL
½ CUP SUGAR	125 mL
PINCH SALT	
2 TBSP. BUTTER	30 mL

ADD LEMON RIND TO BOILING WATER, REDUCE HEAT AND SIMMER FOR 5 MINUTES. IN A SMALL BOWL, MIX CORNSTARCH, SUGAR AND SALT TOGETHER. ADD WATER GRADUALLY, STIRRING CONSTANTLY. RETURN TO SAUCEPAN AND COOK OVER MEDIUM HEAT FOR 10 MINUTES, UNTIL THICKENED. LOWER HEAT AND COOK 5 MINUTES LONGER. REMOVE FROM HEAT, STIR IN LEMON JUICE AND BUTTER. SERVE WARM. MAKES ABOUT 1½ CUPS.

CRANBERRY CUSTARD PIE

BERRIED TREASURE - THINK THANKSGIVING - THINK CHRISTMAS.

ENOUGH PASTRY FOR DOUBLE-CRUST PIE	
12-OZ. PKG. CRANBERRIES (3¾ CUPS), FROZEN IS FINE	365 g
1 CUP BROWN SUGAR	250 mL
3 TBSP. FLOUR	45 mL
2 TBSP. BUTTER, CUT IN SMALL PIECES	30 mL
1 TSP. CINNAMON	5 mL
¼ TSP. CLOVES	1 mL
1 TSP. VANILLA	5 mL
2 EGGS, SEPARATED	

TO PREPARE PASTRY SHELL: ROLL OUT PASTRY FOR 9" PIE SHELL AND PLACE IN PIE PLATE (CRIMP EDGES LATER). ROLL PASTRY FOR TOP CRUST AND SET ASIDE.

TO MAKE FILLING: IN LARGE BOWL, STIR TOGETHER CRANBERRIES, BROWN SUGAR, FLOUR, BUTTER, CINNAMON, CLOVES AND VANILLA. STIR IN EGG YOLKS UNTIL WELL COMBINED. SPOON CRANBERRY MIXTURE INTO SHELL. CUT REMAINING PASTRY INTO ½" STRIPS AND FORM A LATTICEWORK PATTERN ON TOP OF THE FILLING. CRIMP THE EDGES. BRUSH WITH EGG WHITE AND BAKE AT 425°F FOR 10 MINUTES. REDUCE TEMPERATURE TO 350°F AND BAKE 40 MINUTES MORE. DON'T FORGET THE ICE CREAM.

IF YOU WANT TO RECAPTURE YOUR YOUTH, CUT OFF HIS ALLOWANCE.

JALAPEÑO APPLE PIE

PASTRY FOR 9" PIE SHELL

FILLING

3 TBSP. JALAPEÑO JELLY	45 mL
4 CUPS PEELED, SLICED GRANNY SMITH APPLES	1 L
1 TBSP. LEMON JUICE	15 mL
1 TBSP. SUGAR	15 mL
1 TBSP. FLOUR	15 mL
½ TSP. CINNAMON	2 mL
¼ TSP. NUTMEG	1 mL
2 TBSP. BROWN SUGAR	30 mL
2 TSP. MINCED JALAPEÑO	10 mL

TOPPING

½ CUP SUGAR	125 mL
½ CUP FLOUR	125 mL
¼ CUP BUTTER	60 mL
¾ CUP GRATED MONTEREY JACK CHEESE	175 mL

PREHEAT OVEN TO 350°F. SPREAD PIE CRUST WITH JALAPEÑO JELLY. IN A LARGE BOWL, TOSS APPLES WITH LEMON JUICE. IN A SMALL BOWL, COMBINE SUGAR, FLOUR, CINNAMON, NUTMEG AND BROWN SUGAR. SPRINKLE OVER APPLES, TOSS AND SPOON INTO PASTRY SHELL. SPRINKLE JALAPEÑO PEPPER OVER APPLES. COMBINE TOPPING INGREDIENTS TO FORM CRUMBLY MIXTURE AND SPOON OVER PIE. BAKE 45 MINUTES, OR UNTIL GOLDEN. A LITTLE ICE CREAM WOULDN'T HURT EITHER!

CRUST

½ CUP BUTTER	125 mL
1 CUP FLOUR	250 mL
⅓ CUP SUGAR	75 mL
½ TSP. VANILLA	2 mL

FILLING

⅓ CUP RASPBERRY JAM	75 mL
8-OZ. PKG. CREAM CHEESE	250 g
⅓ CUP SUGAR	75 mL
1 EGG	
½ TSP. VANILLA	2 mL
6 APPLES, PEELED, CORED AND SLICED	
⅓ CUP SUGAR	75 mL
2 TSP. CINAMMON	10 mL

TO MAKE CRUST: CUT BUTTER INTO FLOUR (OR BLEND IN A FOOD PROCESSOR), ADD SUGAR AND VANILLA AND MIX WELL. PRESS MIXTURE INTO 9" SPRINGFORM PAN.

TO MAKE FILLING: PREHEAT OVEN TO 450°F. SPREAD JAM ON TOP OF CRUST. BLEND CREAM CHEESE, SUGAR, EGG AND VANILLA AND POUR EVENLY ON TOP OF JAM. COMBINE APPLES, SUGAR AND CINAMMON AND ARRANGE IN OVERLAPPING PINWHEEL PATTERN ON TOP OF CHEESE MIXTURE. BAKE AT 450°F FOR 10 MINUTES. THEN TURN OVEN TO 400°F AND BAKE FOR 25 MINUTES. REMOVE THE SIDES WHEN COOL. THIS IS BEST SERVED AT ROOM TEMPERATURE.

EASIER-THAN-APPLE PIE

THIS RECIPE CONTINUED FROM PAGE 188.

AND NOW FOR SOMETHING A LITTLE DIFFERENT:

. SUBSTITUTE APRICOT JAM FOR RASPBERRY JAM IN FILLING

. SUBSTITUTE ALMOND EXTRACT FOR VANILLA IN FILLING

. SPRINKLE FLAKED ALMONDS ON TOP BEFORE BAKING

. MELT ½ CUP APRICOT JAM IN MICROWAVE AND DRIZZLE OVER TOP AFTER BAKING.

A MAN WHO CORRECTLY GUESSES A WOMAN'S AGE MAY BE SMART, BUT HE'S NOT VERY BRIGHT.

MIZ VICKY'S TEMPTATION

WE GAVE IN - YOU SHOULD TOO!

¼ CUP DEMERARA SUGAR	60 mL
1 CUP 7% SOUR CREAM	250 mL
2 TBSP. KAHLÚA, OR ANY	30 mL
COFFEE-FLAVORED LIQUEUR	

MIX SUGAR AND SOUR CREAM, STIRRING WELL UNTIL BLENDED. ADD KAHLÚA AND STIR AGAIN. REFRIGERATE OVERNIGHT TO BLEND FLAVORS. SERVE WITH AN ASSORTMENT OF FRESH FRUIT.

APPLE PECAN PHYLLO CRISPS

YES! - A YUMMY SKINNY DESSERT!

SHELLS

2 SHEETS PHYLLO PASTRY	
2 TSP. BUTTER, MELTED	10 mL

FILLING

1/3 CUP BROWN SUGAR	75 mL
1 TSP. GRATED LEMON RIND	5 mL
1 TBSP. LEMON JUICE	15 mL
1/2 TSP. CINNAMON	2 mL
3 CUPS PEELED, SLICED APPLES	750 mL
2 TBSP. CHOPPED TOASTED PECANS	30 mL
ICING SUGAR TO SPRINKLE	

TO PREPARE SHELLS: PREHEAT OVEN TO 400°F. LAY PHYLLO SHEET ON WORK SURFACE AND BRUSH WITH HALF THE BUTTER. USING SCISSORS, CUT INTO 3, 5" WIDE STRIPS. FOLD ENDS IN TO MAKE A RECTANGLE OF 3 LAYERS AND GENTLY MOLD INTO MUFFIN CUPS. REPEAT WITH REMAINING PHYLLO AND BUTTER - MAKES 6 SHELLS. BAKE 5 MINUTES, OR UNTIL GOLDEN. THESE CAN BE STORED IN AN AIRTIGHT CONTAINER FOR UP TO 3 DAYS.

TO PREPARE FILLING: IN A HEAVY SKILLET, HEAT SUGAR, LEMON RIND AND JUICE AND CINNAMON UNTIL BUBBLY. ADD APPLES AND COOK, STIRRING FREQUENTLY FOR 5 MINUTES OR UNTIL TENDER. LET COOL SLIGHTLY. SPOON INTO PREPARED SHELLS. SPRINKLE WITH TOASTED PECANS, THEN ICING SUGAR. SERVES 6.

3 GRAMS FAT PER TART

PICTURED ON OVERLEAF

DACQUOISE CAFÉ - PAGE 202

RHUBARB BREAD PUDDING

5 CUPS CUBED DAY-OLD FRENCH BREAD (1/2 LOAF)	1.25 L
3 CUPS SLICED FRESH OR FROZEN RHUBARB	750 mL
13 1/2-OZ. CAN 2% EVAPORATED MILK	385 mL
1 CUP WATER	250 mL
3 EGGS	
1/2 CUP SUGAR	125 mL
1 TSP. GRATED ORANGE RIND	5 mL
1 TSP. VANILLA	5 mL
1/2 TSP. CINNAMON	2 mL
BROWN SUGAR FOR SPRINKLING	

PREHEAT OVEN TO 350°F. COMBINE BREAD AND RHUBARB IN A GREASED 7" X 11" BAKING DISH. IN BOWL, WHISK TOGETHER MILK, WATER, EGGS, SUGAR, ORANGE RIND, VANILLA AND CINNAMON. POUR EGG MIXTURE EVENLY OVER BREAD MIXTURE AND LET STAND 10 MINUTES. BAKE FOR 50-60 MINUTES, UNTIL A KNIFE COMES OUT CLEAN. SPRINKLE EVENLY WITH BROWN SUGAR AND BROIL 6" FROM HEAT FOR 1-2 MINUTES, UNTIL SUGAR MELTS AND TOP IS GOLDEN. (WATCH CAREFULLY - IT BROWNS QUICKLY.) SERVE WARM. SERVES 6.

— 3.6 GRAMS FAT PER SERVING

WANTED: A MAN SECURE ENOUGH TO DO LAUNDRY, WASH DISHES, VACUUM, DUST, COOK, CLEAN THE BATHROOM AND STRONG ENOUGH TO FOOL AROUND AFTERWARDS.

MARGAREE CRANBERRY PUDDING

A THANKSGIVING TRADITION AT "HEART OF HART'S" BED AND BREAKFAST IN THE MARGAREE VALLEY, CAPE BRETON, NOVA SCOTIA.

PUDDING

½ CUP MOLASSES	125 mL
½ CUP BOILING WATER	125 mL
1½ TSP. BAKING SODA	7 mL
1⅓ CUPS FLOUR	325 mL
1 TSP. BAKING POWDER	5 mL
1½ CUPS CRANBERRIES (FROZEN ARE FINE)	375 mL

SAUCE

1 CUP SUGAR	250 mL
1 CUP CREAM	250 mL
½ CUP BUTTER	125 mL
⅛ TSP. NUTMEG	0.5 mL
½ TSP. VANILLA	2 mL

TO MAKE PUDDING: IN A 2-CUP MEASURING CUP, MEASURE MOLASSES, BOILING WATER AND BAKING SODA. STIR TO MIX WELL; SET ASIDE.

IN A LARGE BOWL, MIX FLOUR, BAKING POWDER AND CRANBERRIES. ADD MOLASSES MIXTURE, MIX WELL AND POUR INTO GREASED MOLD. COVER WITH FOIL, SET IN LARGE POT OR DUTCH OVEN AND ADD WATER HALFWAY UP MOLD. COVER POT AND SIMMER ON LOW HEAT FOR 1½-2 HOURS. CHECK WATER LEVEL PERIODICALLY. REHEAT (STEAM OR MICROWAVE) BEFORE SERVING.
IF YOU'RE REALLY ORGANIZED, MAKE PUDDING AHEAD OF TIME AND FREEZE.

MARGAREE CRANBERRY PUDDING

THIS RECIPE CONTINUED FROM PAGE 194.

TO MAKE SAUCE: COOK ALL INGREDIENTS OVER MEDIUM HEAT UNTIL BOILING. SET ASIDE TO COOL.

TO SERVE: STEAM PUDDING FOR 1 HOUR OR WARM IN MICROWAVE AND SERVE WITH WARM SAUCE.

SINFULLY RICH LOW-FAT FUDGE SAUCE

SERVE OVER FRUIT, ANGEL FOOD CAKE OR LOW-FAT FROZEN YOGURT.

½ CUP SUGAR	125 mL
¼ CUP COCOA	60 mL
4 TSP. CORNSTARCH	20 mL
½ CUP EVAPORATED SKIM MILK	125 mL
2 TSP. VANILLA	10 mL

IN SMALL SAUCEPAN, COMBINE SUGAR, COCOA AND CORNSTARCH. STIR IN MILK AND WHISK OVER LOW HEAT FOR 3 MINUTES, OR UNTIL MIXTURE BOILS. WHISK 1-2 MINUTES LONGER, UNTIL THICKENED AND SMOOTH. REMOVE FROM HEAT AND STIR IN VANILLA. SERVE WARM OR COLD. REFRIGERATE LEFTOVER SAUCE. MAKES 1 CUP.

LESS THAN 2 GRAMS FAT IN 3 TBSP. SAUCE COMBINED WITH ANY OF THE SERVING SUGGESTIONS.

ENGLISH BERRY PUDDING

ORIGINALLY A SUMMER PUDDING OF STEWED AVAILABLE FRUIT - BUT FROZEN BERRIES ARE GOOD YEAR ROUND!! SERVE WITH CRÈME FRAÎCHE OR MAKE THIS A LOW-FAT DESSERT USING MOCK CRÈME FRAÎCHE.

6 CUPS BERRIES, MIXTURE OF	1.5 L
BLUEBERRIES, STRAWBERRIES, AND	
RASPBERRIES (FRESH OR FROZEN)	
GRATED RIND OF 1 LEMON	
½ CUP SUGAR	125 mL
6-8 SLICES WHITE BREAD	
MINT LEAVES TO GARNISH	

CRÈME FRAÎCHE

1 CUP WHIPPING CREAM	250 mL
1 CUP SOUR CREAM	250 mL

MOCK CRÈME FRAÎCHE

½ CUP SKIM MILK YOGURT	125 mL
½ CUP 7% SOUR CREAM	125 mL
2 TBSP. SUGAR	30 mL
1 TSP. VANILLA	5 mL

SLICE STRAWBERRIES IN HALF. COMBINE FRUIT, LEMON RIND AND SUGAR IN SAUCEPAN. COVER AND SIMMER 10-15 MINUTES. REMOVE CRUSTS FROM BREAD SLICES AND CUT BREAD IN HALF. LINE SIDES AND BOTTOM OF ROUND, STRAIGHT-SIDED DISH. STRAIN FRUIT PULP, RESERVE JUICE AND POUR SOME OF JUICE OVER BREAD LINING. ADD HALF THE FRUIT PULP. COVER WITH LAYER

ENGLISH BERRY PUDDING

THIS RECIPE CONTINUED FROM PAGE 196.

OF BREAD, THEN ADD REMAINING FRUIT AND JUICE. COVER PUDDING WITH PLASTIC WRAP. PLACE PLATE ON TOP TO WEIGH PUDDING DOWN. REFRIGERATE 12-24 HOURS. TO SERVE, TURN DISH UPSIDE DOWN AND INVERT PUDDING ONTO SERVING PLATE. GARNISH WITH MINT LEAVES. SERVES 6.

TO MAKE CRÈME FRAÎCHE: MIX WHIPPING CREAM AND SOUR CREAM IN A BOWL. LET STAND AT ROOM TEMPERATURE FOR 6 HOURS. PLACE IN REFRIGERATOR TO SET. WILL KEEP IN REFRIGERATOR FOR 1 WEEK.

TO MAKE MOCK CRÈME FRAÎCHE: BEAT ALL INGREDIENTS UNTIL WELL COMBINED. CHILL SEVERAL HOURS TO BLEND FLAVORS.

3.2 GRAMS FAT PER SERVING WITH MOCK CRÈME FRAÎCHE

I WANT A MAN WHO IS KIND AND UNDERSTANDING. THAT'S NOT TOO MUCH TO ASK OF A MILLIONAIRE.

RASPBERRY CREAM WITH BLUEBERRY COULIS

IF YOU LOVE THE FLAVOR OF CHEESECAKE, YOU'LL ADORE THIS REDUCED-FAT VERSION.

RASPBERRY CREAM

2 - 8-OZ. PKGS. LIGHT CREAM CHEESE	2 - 250 g
½ CUP 7% SOUR CREAM	125 mL
½ CUP SUGAR	125 mL
2 EGGS, SEPARATED	
3 CUPS FRESH OR FROZEN RASPBERRIES, MASHED	750 mL

BLUEBERRY COULIS

1¼ CUPS FROZEN BLUEBERRIES, THAWED	300 mL
⅓ CUP SUGAR	75 mL
2 TBSP. WATER	30 mL
2 TBSP. LEMON JUICE	30 mL

TO MAKE RASPBERRY CREAM: LINE 9" x 5" LOAF PAN WITH WAXED PAPER. IN A LARGE BOWL, BEAT CREAM CHEESE, SOUR CREAM, SUGAR AND EGG YOLKS UNTIL LIGHT AND FLUFFY. BEAT EGG WHITES AND FOLD INTO MIXTURE. FOLD IN MASHED RASPBERRIES. POUR INTO PAN AND SMOOTH TOP. COVER AND FREEZE AT LEAST 6 HOURS, OR UNTIL FIRM. IF FROZEN HARD, REMOVE TO REFRIGERATOR 1 HOUR BEFORE SERVING.

TO MAKE BLUEBERRY COULIS: IN SAUCEPAN, COMBINE BLUEBERRIES, SUGAR AND WATER. BRING TO A BOIL. COOK AND STIR OVER MEDIUM HEAT 2-3 MINUTES. PROCESS IN FOOD PROCESSOR FOR

RASPBERRY CREAM WITH BLUEBERRY COULIS

THIS RECIPE CONTINUED FROM PAGE 198.

1 MINUTE AND POUR THROUGH A FINE SIEVE TO REMOVE SKINS. STIR IN LEMON JUICE AND CHILL. STIR WELL BEFORE SERVING. MAKES ABOUT 1 CUP.

TO SERVE: REMOVE FROM PAN AND CUT INTO 8 SLICES. SPOON BLUEBERRY COULIS ON EACH PLATE AND PLACE RASPBERRY SLICE ON TOP. ADD A COUPLE OF WHOLE RASPBERRIES AND BLUEBERRIES FOR GARNISH. SERVES 8.

15.4 GRAMS FAT PER SERVING

"HOW IN THE WORLD DO YOU MANAGE TO GET YOUR CHILDREN'S ATTENTION?"

"I JUST SIT DOWN AND LOOK COMFORTABLE."

ORANGE ANGEL TORTE

THE EFFECT IS VERY PROFESSIONAL - AND IT TASTES EVEN BETTER!

MERINGUE

1½ CUPS TOASTED PECANS	375 mL
½ CUP SUGAR	125 mL
2 TBSP. CORNSTARCH	30 mL
9 EGG WHITES✳	
1 CUP SUGAR	250 mL
1 TSP. VANILLA	5 mL

ORANGE CREAM

3 CUPS WHIPPING CREAM	750 mL
1 CUP ICING SUGAR	250 mL
3 TBSP. ORANGE LIQUEUR OR ORANGE JUICE	45 mL
1½ TBSP. GRATED ORANGE RIND	22 mL

GARNISH

1 CUP COARSELY CHOPPED TOASTED PECANS	250 mL
FRESH ORANGE SLICES	

TO MAKE MERINGUES: LINE 2 BAKING SHEETS WITH BROWN PAPER OR FOIL. DRAW 2, 8" CIRCLES ON EACH SHEET. PLACE PECANS, ½ CUP SUGAR AND CORNSTARCH IN FOOD PROCESSOR AND PROCESS UNTIL FINELY GROUND. IN A LARGE BOWL, BEAT EGG WHITES UNTIL SOFT PEAKS FORM AND GRADUALLY BEAT IN 1 CUP SUGAR UNTIL STIFF PEAKS FORM. ADD VANILLA. GENTLY FOLD IN NUT MIXTURE. DIVIDE MIXTURE AMONG

ORANGE ANGEL TORTE

THIS RECIPE CONTINUED FROM PAGE 200.

THE 4 CIRCLES AND SPREAD EVENLY TO EDGES. BAKE IN CENTRE OF OVEN AT 250°F FOR 1 HOUR. TURN OFF OVEN AND LEAVE OVERNIGHT. (DON'T PEEK!) PEEL PAPER FROM MERINGUES AND SET ASIDE.

TO MAKE ORANGE CREAM: WHIP CREAM, ICING SUGAR AND ORANGE LIQUEUR. STIR IN ORANGE RIND.

TO ASSEMBLE TORTE: SEVERAL HOURS BEFORE SERVING, SPREAD 2/3 OF ORANGE CREAM BETWEEN MERINGUE LAYERS. SPREAD REMAINING CREAM OVER TOP AND SIDES OF TORTE. PRESS PECANS INTO SIDES AND DECORATE TOP WITH ORANGE SLICES. STORE IN REFRIGERATOR.

* TO USE LEFTOVER EGG YOLKS, MAKE "AFTER MERINGUE COOKIES" ("WINNERS" PAGE 157).

THE PROBABILITY OF SOMEONE WATCHING YOU IS PROPORTIONAL TO THE STUPIDITY OF YOUR ACTION.

A CLASSIC FRENCH DESSERT FOR THE NEXT TIME YOU WANT TO SHOW OFF. THE ONLY THING YOU NEED IS A PIPING BAG - AND NO TALENT!

MERINGUE

1½ CUPS FINELY GROUND TOASTED HAZELNUTS (FILBERTS)	375 mL
1 TBSP. CORNSTARCH	15 mL
6 EGG WHITES	
¼ TSP. CREAM OF TARTAR	1 mL
¾ CUP SUGAR	175 mL

MOCHA FILLING

6 EGG YOLKS	
1 TBSP. INSTANT COFFEE GRANULES	15 mL
2 TSP. VANILLA	10 mL
½ CUP SUGAR	125 mL
¼ CUP COCOA POWDER	60 mL
¾ CUP BUTTER, SOFTENED	175 mL

CREAM FILLING

1 CUP WHIPPING CREAM	250 mL
2 TBSP. ICING SUGAR	30 mL
1 TSP. VANILLA	5 mL
ICING SUGAR TO DUST TOP	
WHOLE HAZELNUTS (FILBERTS) TO DECORATE	

TO MAKE MERINGUE: IN A SMALL BOWL, COMBINE HAZELNUTS AND CORNSTARCH. IN A LARGE BOWL BEAT EGG WHITES AND CREAM OF TARTAR UNTIL SOFT PEAKS FORM. GRADUALLY ADD SUGAR (THE SLOWER, THE BETTER), BEATING UNTIL STIFF PEAKS FORM. FOLD IN NUT MIXTURE. COVER 2 BAKING SHEETS WITH FOIL OR BROWN PAPER.

THIS RECIPE CONTINUED FROM PAGE 202.

DRAW 2, 9" CIRCLES AND SPREAD MERINGUE OVER CIRCLES. BAKE IN A 275°F OVEN FOR 1 HOUR THEN TURN OFF OVEN AND LEAVE MERINGUES IN OVEN OVERNIGHT. PEEL OFF FOIL AND SET ON PLATE UNTIL READY TO ASSEMBLE.

TO MAKE MOCHA FILLING: IN A LARGE BOWL, STIR TOGETHER EGG YOLKS, COFFEE GRANULES AND VANILLA. LET STAND 5 MINUTES TO DISSOLVE COFFEE. STIR IN SUGAR AND COCOA AND BEAT 4 MINUTES. ADD BUTTER, 1 TBSP. AT A TIME, BEATING UNTIL FLUFFY. CHILL 1 HOUR TO FIRM SLIGHTLY. (AT THIS POINT, YOU'RE ALLOWED TO TAKE AN "OPRAH" BREAK!)

TO MAKE CREAM FILLING: BEAT WHIPPING CREAM, ICING SUGAR AND VANILLA UNTIL SOFT PEAKS FORM.

PLACE 1 MERINGUE ON A SERVING PLATE. PIPE HALF OF MOCHA FILLING IN A BORDER AROUND THE OUTSIDE EDGE OF THE MERINGUE - THIS IS A GOOD TIME TO PRACTICE BEFORE YOU DO THE TOP. FILL THE CENTER WITH THE CREAM FILLING. TOP WITH SECOND MERINGUE AND SPRINKLE WITH ICING SUGAR. PIPE REMAINING MOCHA FILLING AROUND THE EDGE IN A CONTINUOUS SQUIGGLE. GARNISH WITH WHOLE HAZELNUTS AND CHILL UNTIL SERVING TIME. SERVES 8-10.
(PICTURED ON PAGE 191.)

MOCHA PAVLOVA

OUR LOW-FAT VERSION OF AN OLD FAVORITE

4 EGG WHITES	
¼ TSP. CREAM OF TARTAR	1 mL
½ CUP WHITE SUGAR	125 mL
½ TSP. VANILLA	2 mL
2 TSP. CORNSTARCH	10 mL
1 TBSP. INSTANT COFFEE POWDER	15 mL
½ CUP WHITE SUGAR	125 mL
2 CUPS LOW-FAT WHIPPED TOPPING	500 mL
CINNAMON AND COCOA	
FRESH FRUIT: KIWI FRUIT, STRAWBERRIES, FRESH BLUEBERRIES	
¼ CUP TOASTED SLICED ALMONDS	60 mL

PREHEAT OVEN TO 250°F. BEAT EGG WHITES WITH CREAM OF TARTAR UNTIL FROTHY. GRADUALLY ADD SUGAR BEATING UNTIL STIFF. BEAT IN VANILLA. IN A SMALL BOWL, COMBINE CORNSTARCH, COFFEE POWDER AND SUGAR. FOLD INTO BEATEN EGG WHITES. SPREAD ON WAXED PAPER OR BROWN PAPER ON A PIZZA PAN. MAKE THE CIRCLE SMALLER THAN DESIRED SIZE AS THE BAKED MERINGUE WILL SPREAD. BAKE 1 HOUR, TURN OFF OVEN AND LEAVE OVERNIGHT. (TAPE THE OVEN DOOR - SOMEONE MIGHT DECIDE TO PEEK!) SEVERAL HOURS BEFORE SERVING, COVER WITH WHIPPED TOPPING. JUST BEFORE SERVING, SPRINKLE WITH CINNAMON AND COCOA. ADD FRUIT AND TOASTED ALMONDS. DON'T DESPAIR - THE MERINGUE WILL CRUMBLE WHEN IT'S CUT. SERVES 8.

5.1 GRAMS FAT PER SERVING

MOCHA MOUSSE

CAN YOU BELIEVE IT - LOW FAT!

1/3 CUP SUGAR	75 mL
1/4 CUP COCOA	60 mL
1 ENVELOPE UNFLAVORED GELATIN (1 TBSP.)	15 mL
3/4 TSP. INSTANT COFFEE GRANULES	4 mL
13 1/2-OZ. CAN EVAPORATED SKIM MILK (DIVIDED)	385 mL
1 TSP. VANILLA	5 mL

IN SMALL SAUCEPAN, MIX TOGETHER SUGAR, COCOA, GELATIN AND INSTANT COFFEE GRANULES. STIR IN 3/4 CUP EVAPORATED MILK. ALLOW TO SIT 2 MINUTES. POUR REMAINING 3/4 CUP MILK INTO LARGE BOWL AND PLACE IN FREEZER UNTIL MILK BEGINS TO FREEZE AROUND EDGES. COOK COCOA MIXTURE OVER MEDIUM HEAT STIRRING CONSTANTLY FOR 2-3 MINUTES UNTIL SMOOTH AND GELATIN HAS COMPLETELY DISSOLVED. POUR INTO MEDIUM BOWL, STIR IN VANILLA AND COOL TO ROOM TEMPERATURE, STIRRING OCCASIONALLY. BEAT CHILLED MILK ON HIGH UNTIL SOFT PEAKS FORM. ADD COCOA MIXTURE, STIRRING GENTLY UNTIL WELL BLENDED. POUR INTO INDIVIDUAL DESSERT DISHES. REFRIGERATE UNTIL READY TO SERVE. SERVES 8.

LESS THAN 1 GRAM OF FAT PER SERVING

IN ORDER TO GET A LOAN, YOU MUST FIRST PROVE YOU DON'T NEED IT.

WHISKEY FLIP

REALLY REFRESHING - SERVE IN PARFAIT
GLASSES OR SMALL DESSERT DISHES.

3 EGGS, SEPARATED	250 mL
1 CUP SUGAR, DIVIDED	125 mL
1 LIME, JUICE AND GRATED RIND	
½ CUP RYE WHISKEY	125 mL
⅛ TSP. CREAM OF TARTAR	0.5 mL
1 CUP WHIPPING CREAM	250 mL
MINT LEAVES AND SOME LIME RIND TO GARNISH	

IN A LARGE BOWL, BEAT EGG YOLKS AND ½ CUP
SUGAR UNTIL CREAMY. ADD LIME JUICE, MOST OF
RIND (SAVE SOME FOR GARNISH) AND WHISKEY. IN
A SMALL BOWL, BEAT EGG WHITES UNTIL PEAKS
START TO FORM, ADD CREAM OF TARTAR AND
BEAT UNTIL PEAKS ARE STIFF. FOLD EGG WHITE
MIXTURE INTO YOLK MIXTURE. BEAT CREAM WITH
REMAINING SUGAR UNTIL STIFF. FOLD INTO EGG
MIXTURE AND POUR INTO INDIVIDUAL GLASSES.
FREEZE 4 HOURS OR OVERNIGHT. REMOVE FROM
FREEZER AND PLACE IN REFRIGERATOR 1 HOUR
BEFORE SERVING. GARNISH WITH A MINT LEAF
AND A SPRINKLE OF LIME RIND. SERVES 4-6.

IT'S TRUE THE EARLY BIRD GETS THE WORM, BUT
WHAT DOES THAT SAY ABOUT THE EARLY WORM?

MARGUARITA FRUIT COCKTAIL

RUB THE RIMS OF GLASS DESSERT GOBLETS WITH LIME JUICE AND DIP INTO SUGAR. SERVE WITH CITRUS CRISPS (PAGE 170).

1 SMALL CANTALOUPE, CUT IN CHUNKS OR BALLS	
1 SMALL HONEYDEW MELON, CUT IN CHUNKS OR BALLS	
2 ORANGES, PEELED AND SECTIONED	
1 SMALL GRAPEFRUIT, PEELED AND SECTIONED	
1 MANGO, PEELED AND DICED	
2 CUPS HALVED STRAWBERRIES	500 mL
1/2 CUP SUGAR	125 mL
1/3 CUP ORANGE JUICE	75 mL
3 TBSP. TEQUILA	45 mL
3 TBSP. ORANGE LIQUEUR	45 mL
3 TBSP. FRESHLY SQUEEZED LIME JUICE	45 mL
1 LIME TO RUB RIMS OF GOBLETS	
SUGAR TO DIP GLASSES	

COMBINE FRUIT AND SET ASIDE. IN A SMALL SAUCEPAN, COOK SUGAR AND ORANGE JUICE OVER MEDIUM HEAT FOR 3 MINUTES, UNTIL SUGAR DISSOLVES. REMOVE FROM HEAT, STIR IN TEQUILA, LIQUEUR AND LIME JUICE. COOL AND POUR OVER FRUIT. COVER AND REFRIGERATE 2 HOURS OR OVERNIGHT. MAKES 8 SERVINGS.

 0.7 GRAMS FAT PER SERVING

CHILDREN ARE A GREAT COMFORT TO YOU IN YOUR OLD AGE - AND THEY HELP YOU REACH IT FASTER TOO.

VANILLA PEACH SHERBET

WORTH THE EFFORT! LIGHTER AND CREAMIER THAN REGULAR SHERBET. FREEZE EXTRA PEACHES AND ENJOY THIS DELICIOUS DESSERT IN JANUARY.

1½ CUPS PEELED, SLICED PEACHES (3 MEDIUM)	375 mL
1 TBSP. FRESH LEMON JUICE	15 mL
½ CUP 2% MILK	125 mL
1 TSP. VANILLA	5 mL
¾ CUP SUGAR	175 mL
½ CUP WATER	125 mL
2 EGG WHITES, ROOM TEMPERATURE	

IN A FOOD PROCESSOR OR BLENDER, PURÉE PEACHES AND LEMON JUICE. TRANSFER TO A BOWL AND STIR IN MILK AND VANILLA. CHILL COVERED FOR 30 MINUTES. IN A SMALL SAUCEPAN, COMBINE SUGAR WITH WATER AND BRING TO BOIL, STIRRING OCCASIONALLY. COOK OVER MEDIUM HIGH HEAT WITHOUT STIRRING UNTIL SYRUP REACHES THE SOFT BALL STAGE (240°F - USE YOUR HANDY DANDY CANDY THERMOMETER) - THIS WILL TAKE 3-5 MINUTES. REMOVE SYRUP FROM HEAT AND SET ASIDE. CARRY ON - YOU'LL BE SO GLAD YOU DID! BEAT EGG WHITES UNTIL SOFT PEAKS FORM. RETURN SYRUP TO HEAT UNTIL IT BOILS (YES - YOU HAVE TO DO IT AGAIN!) AND DRIZZLE INTO EGG WHITES (BUT NOT DIRECTLY ONTO THE BEATERS) BEATING CONSTANTLY UNTIL

VANILLA PEACH SHERBET

THIS RECIPE CONTINUED FROM PAGE 208.

EGG WHITES ARE COOL AND VERY STIFF, ABOUT 5 MINUTES. GENTLY COMBINE EGG WHITE MIXTURE AND FRUIT PURÉE AND FREEZE IN AN ICE CREAM MAKER OR - POUR INTO METAL CAKE PAN AND FREEZE UNTIL ALMOST SOLID (ABOUT 6 HOURS - YOU NEEDED A BREAK ANYWAY). NOW, PUT SHERBET BACK IN FOOD PROCESSOR AND MIX UNTIL SMOOTH. RETURN TO FREEZER. STORE IN COVERED CONTAINER IN FREEZER UP TO 10 DAYS. SERVES 6.

 LESS THAN 1 GRAM FAT PER SERVING

MOST MEN START OUT IN LIFE EXPECTING TO FIND A POT OF GOLD AT THE END OF THE RAINBOW. BY THE TIME THEY REACH MIDDLE AGE, MOST OF THEM HAVE AT LEAST FOUND THE POT.

THAT'S TRUMP INDEX

FAT-REDUCED RECIPES ARE INDICATED BY AN ASTERISK

BRUNCH 'N' LUNCH

BEST BUFFETS

SALADS

CHICKEN
- *BARBECUED THAI ... 46
- CAESAR WITH JALAPEÑO ... 50
  LIME DRESSING
- FIESTA TORTILLA ... 45
- GRILLED & SPINACH ... 48

CURRIED RICE ... 52

DRESSING
- *BALSAMIC POPPY SEED ... 65
- ITALIAN ... 67
- *VINAIGRETTE, BALSAMIC ... 66

GREEN BEAN & ROASTED ONION ... 59

POTATO, FRENCH ... 58

ROASTED RED PEPPER ... 49

*SALSA MOLD ... 65

*SANTA FE ... 60

SEAFOOD WITH TARRAGON ... 55
  MUSTARD DRESSING

SHRIMP, PICKLED CITRUS ... 56

SPINACH
- *FRUIT 'N' ... 64
- WARM WITH APPLES ... 62
  AND BRIE

STRAWBERRY AND CHÈVRE ... 63

TORTELLINI, SHOW-OFF ... 57

*WILD RICE ... 61

SOUPS

*BEEF, VEGETABLE ... 82

*BLACK BEAN, MEXICAN ... 76

*BORSCH, SPRING ... 74

*CHICKEN WITH MATZO BALLS ... 80

GARLIC ... 70

*HALIBUT, JUST FOR THE ... 79

*LENTIL, QUICK ... 75

POTATO AND LEEK ... 73

*RASPBERRY ... 68

*TOMATO, WITH PESTO, FRESH ... 69

*TORTELLINI, HEARTY ... 78

*WAR WONTON ... 81

*ZUPPA DU JOUR ... 77

VEGETABLES

*BAKED MEDITERRANEAN ... 84

*CARROTS, ORANGE SESAME ... 87

*DILLED ... 86

POTATOES
- GRUYÈRE SCALLOPED ... 89
- *LIGHTEN-UP SCALLOPED ... 88

RICE
- BROWN & WILD RICE ... 91
- COCONUT RICE ... 90
- *ORANGE ... 146

*TOMATOES, ZUCCHINI-STUFFED ... 85

SAUCES & SALSAS

*CHUTNEY, HOT PEPPER ... 44
  ORANGE

SALSAS
- *KIWI ... 92
- *ROASTED ORANGE
    PEPPER AND CORN ... 93

SAUCES
- B-B-Q SAUCE ... 95
- CRÈME FRAÎCHE ... 196
- LEMON SAUCE ... 185
- *MOCK CRÈME FRAÎCHE ... 196
- *MUSTARD SAUCE ... 94
- *SINFULLY RICH LOW-FAT ... 195
    FUDGE

PIZZA

CARMELIZED ONION AND ... 99
  CHÈVRE

FAST AND EASY CRUST ... 96

MARINATED SUN-DRIED ... 101
  TOMATOES

MEXICAN ... 102

ORIENTAL CHICKEN ... 104

PEAR AND CAMBOZOLA ... 97

PESTO ... 98

PRIMAVERA ... 100

PASTA

*ALFREDO, ACCEPTABLE	109
BALSAMIC	112
FETTUCCINE	
- *ASPARAGUS & SHRIMP	117
- LEMON	107
- SAMBUCA & CRANBERRIES	115
GORGONZOLA	108
LASAGNE	
- CHICKEN TORTILLA	120
- MEXICAN	156
- VEGETABLE	119
*LIGHT VEGGIE	114
*PUTTANESCA	116
*SHRIMP AND FRESH TOMATO	118
SPINACH AND FETA	113
TOMATO & CHEESE, FRESH	111
TORTELLINI WITH THREE CHEESES	110

CHICKEN

*AMARETTO	122
*BARE-NAKED	121
*BREASTS, ZELDA	125
FINGERS	129
*GRILLED LEMON HERB	128
*MEDALLIONS WITH SPINACH	126
PHEASANT	
- CASSEROLE	133
- PIE	134
QUESADILLA, EL GRANDO	29
*SZECHUAN	130
THIGH CHICKEN	132
TORTILLA LASAGNE	120

BEEF

CASSEROLE FOR A COLD NIGHT	157
*FLANK STEAK, GINGER GARLIC	149
*PIE, SKILLET CHILI	154
*STEAK, MEXICAN ROUNDUP	151
STIR-FRY, BULGOGI (KOREAN)	150
TENDERLOIN WITH PEPPERCORN SAUCE	148
TOURTIÈRE	152
*VEAL WITH ARTICHOKES	147

LAMB & PORK

LAMB	
- SOUVLAKI	158
- STEW, GREEK	159
PORK	
- CUTLETS, CAJUN	163
- ROAST, LOIN WITH APPLE TOPPING	161
- STUFFED	162
- TENDERLOIN-WITH HONEY-GLAZED APPLES	160

FISH & SEAFOOD

*ORANGE ROUGHIE POLYNESIAN	138
*RED SNAPPER PARMESAN	139
*SALMON, POACHED WITH PIQUANT SAUCE	136
SHRIMP	
- *ORANGE STIR-FRIED	144
- RICE AND ARTICHOKE CASSEROLE	140
*TUNA, LAYERED CASSEROLE	143

COMBINED INDEX

FAT-REDUCED RECIPES ARE INDICATED BY AN ASTERISK

B - BEST OF BRIDGE
E - ENJOY!
W - WINNERS
G - GRAND SLAM
A - ACES
T - THAT'S TRUMP

CURRIED CHUTNEY SPREAD	43	T
CURRIED SCALLOPS	44	E
CURRIED SEAFOOD COCKTAIL PUFFS	43	E
CURRY DIP FOR VEGETABLES	45	E
DILLED OYSTER CRACKERS	56	G
EMPANADAS	32	A
FLATBREAD, SEASONED	30	A
GUACAMOLE CHERRY TOMATO HALVES	37	W
HAM & CHEESE BALL	49	E
HAM & CHEESE PUFFS	64	G
JALAPEÑO PEPPER JELLY	55	W
JELLY BALLS	44	W
*JEZEBEL	43	T
LOBSTER DIP	48	E
MUSHROOM		
- HOT TURNOVERS	47	W
- SPINACH-STUFFED	52	W
- STUFFED CAPS	63	B
MUSSEL CREOLE	54	G
NACHOS, SUPER	48	W
NUTS & BOLTS	45	G
OYSTERS		
- CADILLAC	38	W
- SMOKED SPREAD	47	G
PASADENA PINWHEELS	38	A
PÂTÉ		
- COUNTRY	70	B
- JOHNNY'S MOMMY'S	47	E
- LIVER	69	B
- SALMON	53	G
- STILTON	37	T
PEACHY CHEESE DIP	34	A
PEPPER JELLY TURNOVERS	42	A
PEPPER RELISH	56	W
PESTO CHEESE BUNDLES	45	A
PETITE PASTIES	48	A
PICANTE SALSA	37	A
PIZZA, STACKED	43	A
PURK'S POO-POOS	53	E
QUESADILLAS		
- EL GRANDO CHICKEN	29	T

- BRIE AND PAPAYA	34	T
- CHEESE	46	A
QUICHE LORRAINE TARTS	68	B
RAILROAD DIP	52	W
RAREBIT-IN-A-HOLE	46	G
RUMAKI	51	E
SALMON		
- SMOKED	53	E
- SMOKED SUPERB	50	W
SEAFOOD		
- HOT DIP	73	B
- WINE	62	G
SHRIMP		
- CRUNCHY	49	E
- DIP	54	E
- MOLDED DIP	37	T
- PICKLED	74	B
SOURDOUGH, "GREY CUP"	31	T
SPANAKOPITA	58	G
SPINACH		
- BITES	41	A
- SPRINGTIME DIP	49	W
SWISS BACON PLEASERS	38	T
TAPENADE	42	T
*TZATZIKI	41	T
WONTON CRISPIES	39	T
ZUCCHINI SQUARES	38	T

BEEF

BONES	120	E
CORNED BEEF & VEGGIES	98	A
GROUND BEEF		
- BEAN STUFF	96	B
- BURGER, CAESAR	102	A
- BURRITOS	113	G
- CABBAGE ROLL CASSEROLE	114	G
- CABBAGE ROLLS	96	W
- CASSEROLE FOR A COLD NIGHT	157	T
- CHINESE	113	B
- ENCHILADAS	126	E

BEEF CONTINUED

GROUND BEEF CONTINUED
- FANDANGO — 137 E
- GOULASH — 131 E
- MEXICAN LASAGNE — 156 T
- *PIE, SKILLET CHILI — 154 T
- SATURDAY NIGHT — 103 B
- SLOPPY JOE POTATOES — 105 A
- TACO PIE — 115 G
- TOURTIÈRE — 88 B
- TOURTIÈRE — 152 T

MEATBALLS
- JELLY BALLS — 44 W
- ORIENTAL — 94 B
- STROGANOFF — 140 E

MEAT LOAF
- FAMILY FAVORITE — 107 W
- MAJOR GREY'S — 101 A

LIVER STIR-FRY — 119 G

RIBS
- SHORT, IN BEER — 151 E
- GRILLED KOREAN — 107 A

ROASTS
- ENGLISH SPICED — 150 E
- UNATTENDED — 123 G

STEAK
- BAKED — 100 B
- BEEF-ON-A-STICK — 103 W
- BEEF & BURGUNDY — 112 E
- BULGOGI — 150 T
- CHATEAUBRIAND WITH COGNAC — 100 A
- CHINESE — 97 B
- EXTRAORDINAIRE WITH SAUCE DIANNE — 118 G
- FAJITAS — 106 A
- *FLANK, GINGER GARLIC — 149 T
- FLANK, SUPER — 104 W
- GINGER FRIED — 120 G
- KABOBS, MUSHROOM — 119 W
- *MEXICAN ROUNDUP — 151 T
- SAUERBRATEN — 111 W
- STROGANOFF GINGER'S — 136 E
- SZECHUAN WITH BROCCOLI — 110 A

BEEF CONTINUED

- TENDERLOIN WITH PEPPERCORN SAUCE — 148 T

STEWING BEEF
- STONED — 154 E
- STROGANOFF — 116 G

VEAL
- MUSHROOMS — 117 W
- 'N' VERMOUTH — 99 A
- OSSO BUCO MILANESE — 108 A
- SCALLOPINI — 142 E
- *WITH ARTICHOKES — 147 T

BEVERAGES

- A REAL SMOOTHIE — 44 G
- BREAKFAST, BLENDER — 12 E
- *BLENDER BREAKFAST — 6 T
- BRANDY
  - COFFEE FREEZE — 14 E
  - MINT CREAM — 60 B
- EGGNOG SUPREME — 59 B
- FALLEN ANGELS — 27 T
- FUZZY NAVELS — 43 G
- GLOGG — 42 G
- HELLO SUNSHINE! — 14 E
- LEMONADE
  - BLENDER — 58 B
  - CONCENTRATE — 60 B
- MARGUARITAS — 15 W
- MID-SUMMER MADNESS — 19 W
- MONGOLIAN DINGBATS — 11 E
- MORNING FLIP, GERRY'S — 11 E
- ORANGE JULIUS — 15 W
- PUNCH
  - GRADUATION — 14 W
  - TERRY'S — 19 W
  - WINTER — 13 E
- RUM
  - BUTTERED, HOT — 43 G
  - CANADIENNE, HOT — 10 E
  - DAIQUIRI — 10 E
  - PEACH FROSTY — 27 T
- SKIP AND GO NAKED! — 12 E

BEVERAGES CONTINUED

TEA

- BLUEBERRY	13	E
- LONG ISLAND ICED	44	G
- SPICED	58	B
SANGRIA	16	W

BREADS

*BAGUETTE, SUE'S x TWO	23	T
BANANA		
- BEST EVER	21	G
- BLUEBERRY	20	G
- GOING	24	W
BISCUITS		
- BUTTERMILK	21	W
- FLAKY FREEZER	28	A
- SAVORY CHEDDAR	26	T
BLUEBERRY COFFEE CAKE	18	E
BREAD		
- APRICOT, L'IL RED'S	26	E
- BROWN, STEAMED	31	W
- CHEDDAR BEER	25	A
- COFFEE CAN	17	E
- COUNTRY CORN	29	W
- FOCACCIA, OLIVE, ONION & ROSEMARY	24	T
- FRENCH, DRESSED UP	32	G
- GARLIC, PARMESAN	16	B
- GINGER	19	E
- HERB	16	B
- JIFFY ORANGE	15	B
- MAPLE SYRUP GRAHAM	30	W
- MOLASSES BROWN	23	G
- NAAN	32	W
- OATMEAL	20	W
- ORANGE HONEY	16	E
- SEASONED FLAT	30	A
- STRAWBERRY	22	G
- TOMATO SAVORY	24	A
BUNS		
- CHEESY	32	G
- CINNAMON	29	A
- IRISH PAN	14	B
- SOUR CREAM GINGER	22	W

BREADS CONTINUED

CRESCENTS, LEMON CREAM	27	A
FERGOSA	24	E
JALAPEÑO CORN STICKS	25	W
LOAVES		
- CHRISTMAS, CARROT	12	B
- CINNAMON	26	A
- LEMON	22	E
- PINEAPPLE	23	W
- PUMPKIN	20	E
- ZUCCHINI	25	E
MELBA HERB TOASTS	25	T
NEW ORLEANS STRIPS	11	B
PITA TOASTS	31	G
SCONES, CRANBERRY	15	T
SPICY BREAD STICKS	30	W
TEA SCONES	34	G
TEXAS TOAST	25	T
WELSH CAKES	33	G

BRUNCHES

ASPARAGUS PUFF	136	W
BACON, CAMPTOWN	9	A
BREAKFAST FRUIT KABOBS	7	A
CASSEROLES		
- SEAFOOD	19	G
- STAMPEDE	10	A
- WEEKENDER SPECIAL	12	W
CHEESE SOUFFLÉ	36	E
CHICKEN SCRAMBLE	32	E
CHRISTMAS WIFE SAVER	33	E
CLAFOUTI, PEACH AND BLUEBERRY	7	T
EGGS		
- BAKED	35	E
- FLORENTINE	13	G
- OLÉ	12	G
- OMELETTE, BRIE, FRESH HERB & TOMATO	12	T
- RANCHERO	31	E
- SCOTTY'S NEST EGGS	11	T
- SUNDAY HAM	7	W

BRUNCHES CONTINUED

FRENCH TOAST
- MIDNIGHT ..... 7 G
- RAPHAEL ..... 14 A

LUNCHEON SOUFFLÉ ROLL ..... 88 W

MEDITERRANEAN PIE ..... 6 A

MUFFULETTA ..... 13 T

QUICHE
- CRABMEAT ..... 38 B
- CRUSTLESS ..... 13 W
- LORRAINE ..... 15 G
- SHRIMP & CRAB ..... 40 B
- SWISS APPLE ..... 8 G
- TOMATO, CHEESE & ..... 8 T
  HERB TART

SAUSAGE
- BASHAW BISTRO RING ..... 13 A
- 'N' JOHNNY CAKE ..... 14 G
- PIE ..... 10 G
- SENSATIONAL ROLL ..... 8 W
- WEEKEND SPOUSE SAVER ..... 10 T

STRATA
- CHEESE & TOMATO ..... 10 W
- MEXICAN ..... 8 A

＊SWISS BREAKFAST MUESLI ..... 6 T

CAKES

APPLE
- DUTCH ..... 196 E
- FRESH ..... 170 A
- SOUR CREAM ..... 167 A

APPLESAUCE SPICE ..... 204 B

CHOCOLATE
- CHIFFON ..... 186 W
- DARK ..... 191 G
- GRAND ..... 174 E
- MOUSSE ..... 184 G
- POUNDCAKE ..... 177 E
- SUPER ..... 206 B
- ZUCCHINI ..... 190 W

CHRISTMAS
- CHERRY ..... 165 E
- LIGHT ..... 202 B

CAKES CONTINUED

COFFEE CAKES
- BLUEBERRY ..... 18 E
- CHRISTMAS ..... 23 E
- COCONUT WHIP ..... 191 W
- ＊CRANAPPLE ..... 14 T
- PECAN HOLIDAY ..... 204 A
- SOUR CREAM ..... 27 E

CRATER ..... 194 W

CUPCAKES, BLACK BOTTOM ..... 185 W

CUPCAKES, CHEESECAKE ..... 188 E

FRUIT COCKTAIL ..... 160 B

KARROT'S ..... 162 E

LAZY DAISY ..... 207 B

MOCHA WHIPPED CREAM ..... 196 G

MY LATEST FAVORITE ..... 166 A

ORANGE, ARMENIAN ..... 172 E

PLUM RUM ..... 168 A

POPPY SEED ..... 174 W

POPPY SEED CHIFFON ..... 192 G

PRUNE ..... 203 B

RHUBARB ..... 163 E

WAR ..... 164 E

CONFECTIONS

ALMONDS
- CANDIED ..... 149 B
- ROCA ..... 166 W
- SOYA ..... 55 E

BOURBON BALLS ..... 168 W

CASHEWS OR PECANS
- SPICED ..... 57 E
- CHEWY TOFFEE ..... 173 T
- CRISPIX MIX ..... 175 T

CHOCOLATE
- FUDGE ..... 192 B
- NUTCHOS ..... 174 T
- PEANUT BUTTER BALLS ..... 171 G
- TIGER BUTTER ..... 171 T
- TRUFFLES ..... 165 A
- TURTLES ..... 172 T

CRACKER JACK ..... 176 T

CRAZY CRUNCH ..... 58 E

E-Z POPCORN BALLS ..... 174 T

CONFECTIONS CONT'D

NUTS AND BOLTS	45	G
NUTS, NOVEL	56	E
PEANUT BRITTLE, MICROWAVE	162	G
PEPPERMINT BRITTLE	164	A
TRAIL MIX, TOM'S	57	E
WALNUTS, CARAMELLED	55	E
XMAS TOFFEE	173	T

COOKIES

ALMOND FLORENTINES	167	W
APPLE, FRESH	158	A
B.L.'S	163	G
BISCOTTI	161	A
BOURBON BALLS	168	W
BROWN BAGGER'S SPECIAL	160	W
CHEWY KIDS	158	W
CHOCOLATE		
- CHIP	167	E
- CHIP, SLAB	161	W
- CHOCOLATE CHIP	156	A
- *ESPRESSO COOKIES	168	T
- FATAL ATTRACTIONS	168	G
- FUDGE BALLS	150	B
- MACADAMIA	157	A
- ORANGE, CHIP	159	A
- PEANUT CHEWY BARS	170	W
- SNOWBALLS	148	B
- SKOR BAR	167	T
- TRUFFLE	163	A
CINNAMON, GLAZED BARS	163	W
CITRUS CRISPS	170	T
COCONUT BARS	159	W
COOKIE OF THE MONTH	164	T
DATE-FILLED COOKIES	165	T
DIAMONDS	170	E
FORGOTTEN COOKIES	139	B
GINGER SNAPS	169	G
GRANOLA	155	A
HERMITS	169	E
MACAROONS	164	A
MERINGUE, AFTER	157	W
MISSION CRY BABIES	166	E
MONA'S MOTHER'S	144	B

COOKIES CONTINUED

ONE CUP OF EVERYTHING	166	T
PEANUT BUTTER	165	G
PECAN CRISPS	166	G
PECAN MACAROONS	140	B
PEPPERNUTS	164	W
POPPY SEED	167	G
PRALINES	143	B
RAISIN, SOFT	147	B
SCOTCH SQUARES	165	W
SHORTBREAD	145	B
- BROWN SUGAR	171	T
- CHEESE	146	B
- FRUIT & NUT	168	E
- JEWISH	145	B
- NANNY'S REAL	160	A
- WHIPPED	146	B
SNICKERDOODLES	162	A
SNOWBALLS	148	B
SWEDISH PASTRY	143	B
VANILAS KIFLEI	169	T
WAFER PUFFS	162	W
ZUCCHINI	164	G

CRUSTS & PASTRY

CHOCOLATE WAFER	209	B
GRAHAM CRACKER	209	B
PASTRY, FAIL-PROOF	200	W
PECAN OR WALNUT	205	G
PUFF PASTRY SHELLS	210	B

DESSERTS

A "GRAND CAKE"	174	E
ANGEL FOOD FLAN	154	B
ANGEL MOCHA TORTE	152	B
APPLE BETTY		
- SOCIAL	208	B
- SPIKED	171	W
APPLE		
- EASIER THAN APPLE PIE	188	T
- KUCHEN	201	W
- *PECAN PHYLLO CRISPS	190	T
- ROLL	156	B

APRICOT SMOOCH	189	E
BANANA GINGER LOAF	182	W
BERRY TART, FRESH	202	A
BLUEBERRY		
- BONANZA	200	A
- BUCKLE	198	A
- DELIGHT	184	B
BRANDY SNAPS	158	B
BUTTER BRICKLE	169	B
CARDINAL'S LIME	178	E
CHANTILLY L'ORANGE	187	A
CHEESECAKE	151	B
- CHOCOLATE CARAMEL	207	A
- CUPCAKES	188	E
- *RASPBERRY CREAM	198	T
WITH BLUEBERRY COULIS		
- PUMPKIN	179	G
CHERRIES JUBILEE	168	B
CHERRY ANGEL FOOD	169	A
CHERRY BERRIES	192	W
CHOCOLATE		
- ACES	186	A
- CHEESE TORTE	182	E
- CHIFFON	186	W
- MOCHA MOUSSE	181	E
- *MOCHA MOUSSE	205	T
- *MOCHA PAVLOVA	204	T
- MOCHA TORTE	166	B
- MOCHA TORTE	199	E
- POTS DE CRÈME	193	E
- RASPBERRY TORTE	177	W
- ROLL	190	E
- SABAYON	189	G
- TORTE ROYALE	180	B
- UPSIDE-DOWN CAKE	171	E
- UPSIDE-DOWN FUDGE	189	A
PUDDING		
- WHITE CHOCOLATE	196	A
MOUSSE, RASPBERRY		
CRÈME CARAMEL	188	G
CRÈME DE MENTHE	164	B
DACQUOISE CAFÉ	202	T
DANISH RUM SOUFFLÉ	194	E

DATE TORTE	195	E
FRUIT COCKTAIL CAKE	160	B
*FRUIT COCKTAIL,	207	T
MARGUARITA		
FRUIT POOF	180	W
GRAND MARNIER CRÈME	193	W
GRAND SLAM FINALE	187	G
GRASSHOPPER CAKE	186	E
HAZELNUT TORTE	194	G
LEMON		
- BERRY CAKE	182	B
- FROZEN MOUSSE &	196	W
RASPBERRY SAUCE		
- FROZEN PUFF	185	A
- ICE BOX PUDDING	170	B
- PUDDING	192	E
- SORBET	190	G
- STRAWBERRY ANGEL	174	B
TARTS		
MARSHMALLOW COFFEE	189	B
MELON & RUM SAUCE	198	E
MIZ VICKY'S TEMPTATION	189	T
ORANGE ANGEL TORTE	200	T
PAVLOVA	203	W
PEACH		
- BRANDIED	183	B
- EASY TORTE	195	W
- FLAMBÉ	163	B
- FROSTY	180	G
- *VANILLA PEACH	208	T
SHERBET		
PEPPERMINT		
- CANDY	188	B
- ICE CREAM	185	B
PINEAPPLE SLICE	162	B
PUDDINGS		
- CAJUN BREAD	190	A
- *ENGLISH BERRY	196	T
- GRANDMA'S CHRISTMAS	208	A
- JAKE'S RICE	195	A
- LEMON	192	E
- MARGAREE CRANBERRY	194	T
- *RHUBARB BREAD	193	T

DESSERTS CONTINUED

- UPSIDE-DOWN CHOCOLATE FUDGE	189	A
QUICK FROZEN RASPBERRY	173	B
- *CREAM WITH BLUEBERRY COULIS	198	T
- PECAN TART & SOUR CREAM GLAZE	180	A
RHUBARB		
- COBBLER	205	A
- CREAM	188	W
- CRISP WITH BOURBON SAUCE	182	G
- *RHUBARB BREAD PUDDING	193	T
- RHUBARB DELIGHT	181	G
RUM CAKE	153	B
SABAYON, STELLA	193	G
STRAWBERRY		
- ANGEL FOOD CAKE	187	B
- CRÊPES	178	B
- FRESH DELIGHT	173	E
- LEMON ANGEL TARTS	174	B
- PUFF PANCAKE	172	B
- SHERBET, FRESH	199	A
TIA MARIA CAKE	200	E
TIRAMISU	186	G
TOFFEE MERINGUE	183	G
TRIFLE, ENGLISH	184	E
WHISKEY FLIP	206	T

FISH & SEAFOOD

ARCTIC CHAR, STUFFED	104	E
BAKED FISH MOZZARELLA	127	G
CIOPPINO	129	A
CRAB		
- CASSEROLE	41	B
- CASSEROLE, BAKED	42	B
- CRÊPES	34	B
- CURRIED, TETRAZZINI	110	B
- LUNCHEON SOUFFLÉ	88	W
- QUICHE	38	B
CRUNCHY OVEN-BAKED	134	A

FISH & SEAFOOD CONT'D

HALIBUT		
- CHOWDER	79	T
- GRILLED & PEPPERS JULIENNE	128	A
- ORANGE GINGER	127	A
- WINE POACHED	126	G
LOBSTER NEWBURG	84	B
MARINATED FISH FILLETS WITH BASIL BUTTER	128	G
MUSSELS & SCALLOPS IN CREAM	130	G
ORANGE ROUGHIE DIJONNAISE	126	A
*ORANGE ROUGHIE POLYNESIAN	138	T
OYSTER SCALLOP	106	E
SALMON		
- CHILLED SOUFFLÉ	108	E
- *POACHED WITH PIQUANT SAUCE	136	T
- POTLATCH	129	G
- STEAKS, BAR-B-QUED	105	E
- STEAKS, TERIYAKI	127	G
- STUFFING		
- RICE & OLIVE	106	E
- WILD WEST	125	A
SCALLOPS		
- COQUILLE DAVID	122	E
- IN WINE	85	B
SCALLOPS		
- PAPRIKA	131	A
- SHELLS, SEAFOOD	39	B
SCAMPI	102	E
SEAFOOD		
- CASSEROLE	19	G
- CREAMED	86	B
- CURRY	82	B
- KABOBS	131	G
SHELLFISH PUKÉ	148	E
SHRIMP		
- & CRAB QUICHE	40	B
- & RICE & ARTICHOKES	140	T
- & SCALLOP SUPREME	130	A

FISH & SEAFOOD CONT'D

SHRIMP CONTINUED

- IN FOIL	112	B
- *ORANGE STIR-FRIED	144	T
- PARTY	111	B
- STIR-FRY	132	A
- STROGANOFF	80	B
- SZECHUAN	133	A

SNAPPER

- BAKED ITALIANO	124	A
- CREAMY DILLED	124	G
- *PARMESAN	139	T

SOLE

- BAKED ROULADE	109	E
- O-MIO	125	G
- YOU GOTTA HAVE	102	E
*TUNA, LAYERED CASSEROLE	143	T

FOWL

CHICKEN

- ALMOND	110	E
- *AMARETTO	122	T
- BALLS	78	B
- BARBECUE, MARINADE	139	E
- *BARE-NAKED	121	T
- BRANDIED, SAMS	100	W
- BREASTS, ASPARAGUS	120	A
- BREASTS, STUFFED	102	B
- *BREASTS, ZELDA	125	T
- BURRITOS	114	A
- CANTONESE	133	E
- CASSEROLE	81	B
- ARTICHOKE	87	W
- ENCHILADA	153	G
- MANDALAY	154	G
- MEXICANA	159	G
- 'N' NOODLE	121	E
- POLYNESIAN	79	B
- *SZECHUAN	130	T
- THIGH	132	T
- WILD RICE	152	E
- WINE	107	B
- YUMMY	86	W
- CATCH-A-TORY	152	G
- CHILI, SOUTHWESTERN	116	A

FOWL CONTINUED

- CLASSY	85	W
- CRAB, STUFFED	124	E
- CRÊPES	34	B
- CRISPY SESAME	146	G
- DIVINE, DIVAN	138	E
- ENCHILADAS	110	W
- FAJITAS, TEX MEX	106	A
- FINGERS	129	T
- FRIED RICE	98	B
- *GRILLED LEMON HERB	128	T
- HONEY MUSTARD	113	A
- JAMBALAYA	153	E
- KABOBS	141	A
- LASAGNE	114	W
- LEMON	111	E
- LIME GRILLED	119	A
- MAPLE-ORANGE	118	A
- *MEDALLIONS	126	T
- ORANGE ROSEMARY	111	A
- OVEN-FRIED	117	A
- PARMESAN	149	G
- POT PIE	155	G
- QUESADILLA, EL GRANDO	29	T
- STICKY BAKED	115	A
- SWEET 'N' SPICY CASHEW	148	G
- TETRAZZINI	92	W
- TORTILLA LASAGNE	120	T
- WHIPLASH	156	G
- WINGS		
- CURRIED	109	B
- JAPANESE	106	B

CORNISH HENS — 150 G

DUCK

- BREAST EN CASSEROLE	147	G
- ROAST, WITH ORANGE SAUCE	146 / 147	E / E

PHEASANT

- ALMOND ORANGE	150	G
- CASSEROLE	133	T
- MADEIRA	123	A
- PIE	134	T

FOWL CONTINUED

STUFFING
- TURKEY, TERRIFIC .... 40 G
TURKEY CASSEROLE .... 108 B

ICING & DESSERT SAUCES

DRESSING
- FRESH FRUIT .... 206 G
- FRUIT DIP .... 206 G
- POPPY SEED .... 119 B

ICING
- FLUFFY .... 160 E
- ISLA'S .... 191 B
- LEMON, FLUFFY .... 20 E
  CREAM TOPPING
- VANILLA, CREAMY .... 191 B
  FROSTING

SAUCES
- *BLUEBERRY COULIS .... 198 T
- CRÈME FRAÎCHE .... 196 T
- DELUXE .... 190 B
- FOAMY BUTTER .... 191 E
- FUDGE .... 191 E
- FUDGE, HOT .... 173 W
- GOLDEN .... 208 A
- LEMON .... 185 T
- *MOCK CRÈME FRAÎCHE .... 196 T
- RASPBERRY .... 196 A
- RUM .... 190 A
- *SINFULLY RICH FUDGE .... 195 T

LAMB

CURRY .... 136 A
LEG, RED CURRANT .... 84 W
MARINATED, BARBECUED .... 116 W
MOUSSAKA .... 108 W
RACK, MUSTARD COATING .... 137 A
SOUVLAKI .... 158 T
STEW, GREEK .... 159 T

MUFFINS

APPLE CINNAMON .... 21 E
BACK-PACKING .... 21 T
BANANA .... 29 G

MUFFINS CONTINUED

BLUEBERRY, LEMON .... 15 E
BRAN, A PAIL FULL .... 20 A
CARROT & RAISIN .... 27 G
CHEESE
- & BACON .... 28 G
- CHEDDAR APPLE .... 15 A
- CHEDDAR DILL .... 27 W
- CREAM .... 24 G
CRANBERRY .... 16 A
*GUILT-REDUCED BRAN .... 22 T
HEALTH NUT .... 30 G
LUNCH BOX .... 23 A
MINCEMEAT .... 26 W
*MORNING GLORY .... 20 T
OAT .... 13 B
OAT BRAN .... 21 A
ORANGE
- MANDARIN .... 25 G
- SUNSHINE .... 28 W
PIZZA .... 22 A
PUMPKIN PECAN .... 19 A
*RASPBERRY-FILLED .... 19 T
  CINNAMON
RHUBARB, PHANTOM .... 26 G
SCONES, CRANBERRY .... 15 T
STRAWBERRY .... 16 T

PASTA

BALSAMIC .... 112 T
CANNELLONI .... 114 E
CHICKEN, SPAGHETTINI .... 152 A
CRAB & BASIL .... 134 G
FETTUCCINE
- FLORENTINE .... 154 A
- VERDE .... 121 W
- LEMON .... 107 T
- SAMBUCA & CRANBERRIES .... 115 T
- *WITH ASPARAGUS & .... 117 T
  SHRIMP
FRESH TOMATO & CHEESE .... 111 T
LASAGNE .... 104 B
- BROCCOLI .... 145 G
- CHICKEN .... 114 W

PASTA CONTINUED

LASAGNE CONTINUED
- CHICKEN TORTILLA — 120 T
- HAM & MUSHROOM — 136 G
- MEXICAN LASAGNE — 156 T
- PESTO — 146 A
- SEAFOOD — 103 E
- SPINACH — 143 G
- VEGETABLE — 119 T

GORGONZOLA — 108 T

LINGUINI
- CLAM SAUCE — 122 W
- RED CLAM SAUCE — 133 G

MACARONI, GOURMET — 135 G
MANICOTTI — 102 W
NOODLES, SINGAPORE — 112 A
ORZO, PARMESAN & BASIL — 81 A
PASTA POT — 120 W
PENNE - SPICY — 142 G
PEPPERS — 149 A
PEROGY - CASSEROLE — 153 A
PIE — 148 A
PRIMAVERA — 138 G
*PUTTANESCA — 116 T
ROTINI, SHRIMP IN GARLIC CREAM — 151 A

SAUCES
- ALFREDO — 83 W
- *ALFREDO, ACCEPTABLE — 109 T
- ARTICHOKE — 143 A
- CREAMY MUSHROOM — 150 A
- GAFFER'S — 128 E
- ITALIAN SAUSAGE — 132 G
- MINDLESS MEAT — 117 E
- PESTO — 127 W

*SHRIMP AND TOMATO — 118 T

SPAGHETTI
- CARBONARA — 144 G
- WITH EGGPLANT — 114 B

SPINACH AND FETA — 113 T

TORTELLINI
- RED & WHITE — 144 A
- WITH THREE CHEESES — 110 T

*VEGGIE, LIGHT — 114 T

PIES

CHOCOLATE
- BRITTLE — 182 A
- LINCOLN CENTRE — 197 E
- MINT — 157 B
- MOUSSE — 189 W
- MUD — 180 E
- PECAN — 203 G

COFFEE ICE CREAM — 161 B
CRANBERRY CUSTARD — 186 T
FLAPPER — 172 W
FUDGE, CUSTARD SAUCE — 198 G
GRASSHOPPER — 165 B
IRISH COFFEE CREAM — 198 W
JALAPEÑO APPLE — 187 T
LEMON, FRENCH — 201 G
LIME PARFAIT — 173 B
*MINCEMEAT TARTS — 184 T
PALACE — 200 G
PEACHES & CREAM — 197 G
PEANUT BUTTER — 184 A
PECAN — 179 E
PECAN CRUST ICE CREAM & CARAMEL SAUCE — 205 G

PUMPKIN
- CHIFFON — 184 W
- PECAN — 202 W

RHUBARB
- MERINGUE — 204 G
- STRAWBERRY CRUMBLE — 183 A

RUM CREAM — 171 B
SHOO-FLY — 187 W
TIN ROOF — 202 G

PORK

CHINESE — 87 B
CHOP SUEY — 134 E
CHOP SUEY, NOODLE — 112 W
CUTLETS, CAJUN PORK — 163 T
DUMPLINGS — 98 W

HAM
- APRICOTS — 119 E
- BEER — 82 W
- CASSEROLE — 141 E
- JAMBALAYA — 153 E
- LOAF — 161 G

PORK CONTINUED

KABOBS, NO-BRAINER	141	A
MEDALLIONS	138	A
PEACHY	130	E
RIBS		
- DRY	99	B
- GREEK	117	G
- ORANGE SPUNKY	97	W
- SWEET & SOUR	144	E
- SWEET & SOUR CHILI	132	E
ROAST		
- BARBECUED	90	W
- CROWN, APPLE RAISIN STUFFING	142	A
- LOIN	135	A
- LOIN WITH APPLE	161	T
SATAY	129	E
STUFFING		
- APPLE RAISIN	142	A
- CRANBERRY	39	G
TENDERLOIN		
CASHEWS	94	W
STUFFED	162	T
WITH HONEY-GLAZED APPLES	160	T
TOMATO CANTONESE	160	G
TOURTIÈRE	88	B
TOURTIÈRE	152	T

PIZZA

CARAMELIZED ONION & CHÈVRE	99	T
FAST AND EASY CRUST	96	T
MARINATED SUN-DRIED TOMATOES	101	T
MEXICAN	102	T
ORIENTAL CHICKEN	104	T
PEAR AND CAMBOZOLA	97	T
PESTO	98	T
PRIMAVERA	100	T

SALADS

ARTICHOKE		
- MARINATED, MUSHROOM	68	W
- ZUCCHINI	60	W
AVOCADO, FRUIT	127	B
BEET, RUSSIAN	78	G
BROCCOLI, MANDARIN	57	A
CAESAR	121	B
CANLIS	61	E
CHICKEN		
- ASPARAGUS	61	A
- *BARBECUED THAI	46	T
- CAESAR	50	T
- CURRIED BOATS	50	B
- FIESTA TORTILLA	45	T
- FRUIT & LIME	88	G
- GRILLED & SPINACH	48	T
- KOREAN	64	W
- LAYERED	57	W
COLE SLAW		
- KILLER	76	G
- PICKLED	60	E
- PINEAPPLE	128	B
COMMITTEE	66	W
CUCUMBER, LEE HONG'S	64	E
CURRIED RICE	52	T
FOO YUNG, TOSSED	65	E
FRENCH POTATO	58	T
FRUIT		
- ARIZONA	86	G
- AVOCADO	127	B
- MANDARIN ORANGE	71	E
- MARINATED	89	G
- *'N' SPINACH	64	T
- PAPAYA AVOCADO	51	A
- PEAR & WALNUT	50	A
- SUNSHINE	60	A
- WALDORF	120	B
- YUCATÁN	58	A
GREEK	70	W
GREEN BEAN & ONION	59	T
LAYERED	69	E
MEXICAN CHEF	46	B

SALADS CONTINUED

MOLDED
- CHICKEN ATLANTA   62 W
- CHICKEN GUMBO   56 B
- COTTAGE CHEESE   57 B
- CUCUMBER CREAM   62 E
- EGGNOG   49 A
- FRUIT COCKTAIL   55 B
- HORSERADISH   117 B
- LOBSTER MOUSSE   48 B
- PINK FROSTY   125 B
- *SALSA MOLD   65 T
- TOMATO ASPIC   52 B

MUSHROOM, HOT   59 W
ORIENTAL GARDEN TOSS   67 W

PASTA
- ASPARAGUS   84 G
- CHINESE NOODLES   62 A
- CRAB 'N' GINGER   64 A
- SALMON   82 G
- SHOW-OFF TORTELLINI   57 T
- VEGETABLE   73 W

PEACHTREE PLAZA   69 W
POTATO, FRENCH   58 T
ROASTED RED PEPPER   49 T

ROMAINE
- DOUBLE GREEN   52 A
- ORANGES & PECANS   80 G

*SANTA FE   60 T

SEAFOOD
- AVOCADO CRAB   44 B
- BUFFET   59 E
- GREEN GODDESS   63 E
- SENATE   45 B
- WITH TARRAGON
    MUSTARD DRESSING   55 T

SHRIMP
- BOATS   47 B
- LOUIS   66 E
- PAPAYA   81 G
- PICKLED CITRUS   56 T
- SALAD   49 B

SALADS CONTINUED

SPINACH
- ARMENIAN   70 E
- DIFFERENT   79 G
- FRESH   116 B
- MELON   56 A
- *'N' FRUIT   64 T
- ROYALE   71 E
- SOUR CREAM   61 W
- STRAWBERRY   55 A
- WARM, APPLES & BRIE   62 T
- WILTED   117 B

STRAWBERRY, CHÉVRE   63 T
SUNOMONO PLATTER   67 E
SUPER   126 B

TOMATO
- MARINATED   118 B
- MOZZARELLA   63 A

VEGETABLE MARINATED   115 B
VINAIGRETTE, WARM   59 A
*WILD RICE   61 T
ZUCCHINI   77 G

SALAD DRESSINGS

*BALSAMIC POPPY SEED   65 T
*BALSAMIC VINAIGRETTE   66 T
BLUE CHEESE   87 G
FRESH FRUIT   83 G
ITALIAN   67 T
JALAPEÑO LIME   50 T
MAYO, DOCTORED   58 W
ORANGE SHERRY   55 A
PESTO   73 W
POPPY SEED   119 B
TARRAGON MUSTARD   55 T
THOUSAND ISLAND   85 G
YOGURT CURRY   52 A

SANDWICHES

ASPARAGUS	28	B
BRIDGE PIZZAS	23	B
COCKTAIL	26	B
CRAB		
- CHEESE BUNS	26	B
- CHEESE TOASTIES	21	B
- DEVILED EGG	21	B
GOURMET TOAST	19	B
GRILLED CHEESE		
- ITALIANO	31	B
- THE UTMOST	16	G
HAM		
- BUNS	32	B
- CHEESE TOWERS	25	B
- FILLED	20	B
- 'N' CHEESE PARTY	29	B
- OPEN FACE	34	B
- SPINACH BAGUETTE	11	A
- STUFFED LOAF	29	E
LOAF, RENE'S	30	B
MUFFELETTA	13	T
PÂTÉ EN BAGUETTE	12	A
REUBEN	27	B
SEAFOOD SALAD	23	B
SHRIMP		
- FAST ROLLS	22	B
- SANDWICHES	28	E
SUNDAY	30	E
TACOS	24	B
TOMATO CHEESIES	34	E
TUNA PIZZA BURGER	33	B

SAUCES & RELISHES

CHUTNEY	134	B
- CRANBERRY & RAISIN	96	A
- HOT PEPPER ORANGE	44	T
JALAPEÑO PEPPER JELLY	55	W
MARMALADE		
- CARROT	94	A
- CHRISTMAS	37	E
- GREEN TOMATO	38	G
MINCEMENT, GREEN TOMATO	97	A
MUSTARD		
- B.L!S PICKLES	95	A
- HOT & SWEET	93	A

SAUCES CONTINUED

MUSTARD		
- MONK'S	130	W
- TARRAGON	131	W
- *SAUCE	94	T
RELISHES		
- CORN	37	G
- GREEN TOMATO	133	B
- PEPPER RELISH	56	W
- PICALILLI	35	G
- PLUM, BLUE	38	E
- RHUBARB	92	B
- ZUCCHINI	126	W
SALSAS		
- *KIWI SALSA	92	T
- *ORANGE PEPPER	93	T
AND CORN		
- SALSA	95	W
- PICANTE	37	A
SAUCES		
- B.B.Q.	95	T
- CHILI	132	B
- CRANBERRY BURGUNDY	136	B
- CRANBERRY GOURMET	38	G
- CUMBERLAND	129	W
- GUACAMOLE	37	W
- HOLLANDAISE, BLENDER	92	A
- GINGER SOY	135	B
- MUSTARD	101	B
- FOR HAM	136	B
- FOR STEAK	101	B
- PEANUT	36	G
- PESTO	127	W
- PLUM	125	W
- TERIYAKI	135	B
SEASONINGS		
- CREOLE	92	A
- FLOUR	41	G
- SALT, SUBSTITUTE	41	G
STUFFINGS		
- APPLE RAISIN	142	A
- CRANBERRY	39	G
- RICE & OLIVE	106	E
- TURKEY, TERRIFIC	40	G
WINE CORDIAL	125	W

SOUPS

AVGOLEMONO	67	G
AVOCADO	68	G
BEAN, BEST OF BRIDGE	73	A
*BEEF VEGETABLE STOCK	82	T
*BLACK BEAN, MEXICAN	76	T
*BORSCH, SPRING	74	T
BROCCOLI	74	W
CARROT	70	A
CAULIFLOWER, BLUE CHEESE	73	G
CHEDDAR CORN CHOWDER	69	A
*CHICKEN & MATZO BALLS	80	T
CLAM CHOWDER	75	E
CRAB BISQUE	76	E
CRAB & CORN CHOWDER	74	E
CREAM OF		
- CRAB	76	E
- CUCUMBER	77	E
- CURRY	75	W
- PARSLEY & BASIL	71	G
- SPINACH	72	G
- TOMATO	67	A
CUCUMBER, CREAM OF	77	E
CURRY, CREAM OF	75	W
EGG DROP	76	W
ELEPHANT	79	E
FISHERMAN'S CHOWDER	77	W
GAZPACHO	130	B
GARLIC	70	T
*HALIBUT, JUST FOR THE, CHOWDER	79	T
HAMBURGER	129	B
HERB, WITH SHRIMP	79	W
*LENTIL, QUICK	75	T
MELON		
- GINGERED	76	W
- TWO-TONE	65	A
MINESTRONE	73	E
- TUSCAN	72	A
MULLIGATAWNY	66	G
MUSHROOM	78	W
- & LEEK	75	G
ONION, FRENCH	81	W
OYSTER STEW	131	B

SOUPS CONTINUED

PARSLEY, CREAM OF	71	G
PEA, HABITANT	78	E
POTATO	74	G
POTATO & LEEK	73	T
PUMPKIN	71	A
*RASPBERRY	68	T
RED PEPPER	68	A
SPINACH, CREAM OF	72	G
STRAWBERRY, COLD	66	A
TOMATO, CREAM OF	67	A
*TOMATO, FRESH, PESTO	69	T
TOMATO BISQUE, FRESH	80	W
*TORTELINI, HEARTY	78	T
TURKEY	72	E
*WAR WONTON	81	T
*ZUPPA DU JOUR	77	T

SQUARES

APPLE BROWNIES	183	T
BROWNIES	205	B
BROWNIES, FUDGE	161	E
BUTTER TART SLICE	172	G
CARAMEL BARS	157	E
CARAMEL NUT BROWNIES	182	T
CHEESE	195	B
CHOCOLATE		
- CARAMEL	177	A
- CRUNCH BARS	177	T
- PECAN	178	A
- ROCKY MOUNTAIN	173	G
- UNTURTLE BAR	179	T
- VERNA'S	201	B
CRANBERRY	176	A
DREAM SLICE	194	B
FUDGE SCOTCH	192	B
EAT MORE..MORE...MORE...	181	T
GEORGE (NANAIMO)	198	B
JOSHUA'S MOM'S SKATING BARS	180	T
LEMON BARS	158	E
MAGIC COOKIE BARS	196	B
MATRIMONIAL	170	G
MEXICAN WEDDING CAKE	197	B

SQUARES CONTINUED

MRS. LARSON'S BARS	159	E
PEANUT BUTTER		
- BROWNIES	174	G
- CRUNCHIES	197	B
- SLICE	196	B
PECAN SHORTBREAD	206	A
PEPPERMINT BARS	186	B
PUFFED WHEAT	179	A
RASPBERRY	193	B
RASPBERRY WALNUT	175	A
RICE KIRSPIE SQUARES	178	T
TOFFEE KRISPS	178	T

TARTS

BUTTER	200	B
CHEDDAR APPLE	171	A
*MINCEMEAT	184	T
PECAN CUPS	177	G
SHORTBREAD	199	B
TART FILLINGS		
- CHEESE & FRUIT	178	G
- LEMON BUTTER	189	B
- LEMON CHEESE	199	B
- GREEN TOMATO MINCEMEAT	97	A

VEGETABLES

ASPARAGUS		
- BAKED	91	G
- NOODLE BAKE	92	G
- PUFF	136	W
BEANS		
- BAKED	148	W
- CALICO POT	94	G
- GREEN, CASSEROLE	89	E
- GREEN, GUIDO	90	A
- GREEN, MANDARIN	149	W
- GREEN, SUDDEN VALLEY	145	W
- GREEN, VINAIGRETTE	89	A
- SPEEDY, BAKED	95	G

VEGETABLES CONTINUED

BROCCOLI		
- CASSEROLE	100	E
- EASTER	85	E
- RICE CASSEROLE	95	E
- SESAME	96	E
- SICILIAN	92	G
- TIMBALES	100	G
- WILD RICE	93	B
BRUSSELS SPROUTS		
- SAUCY	88	A
- TOLERABLE	134	W
CABBAGE		
- FRIED	95	G
- RED	91	E
CARROTS		
- GRAPES, GLAZED	150	W
- L'ORANGE	153	W
- NIFTY	143	W
- *ORANGE SESAME	87	T
- PATCH	84	A
- WITH ARTICHOKES	83	A
CAULIFLOWER, CURRIED	96	G
CELERY SAUTÉ	75	A
CHILI, BARBER'S BEST	76	A
CHILIES RELLENOS	132	W
CORN		
- DEVILED	84	E
- SOUFFLÉ	80	E
*DILLED	86	T
FRUIT		
- BANANAS, BAKED	93	G
- CURRIED, HOT	96	E
GREENS, YEAR ROUND	98	E
*MEDITERRANEAN, BAKED	84	T
MUSHROOMS		
- AU GRATIN	87	A
- FESTIVE	88	E
ONIONS		
- BOOZY	144	W
- BROCCOLI, STUFFED	106	G
- CHEESE, MARINATED	105	G
- PICKLED	101	E
PARSNIPS, PERFECT	108	G

VEGETABLES CONTINUED

PEAS
- CASSEROLE — 83 E
- COLD DILLED — 144 W

PEPPERS
- JULIENNE — 128 A
- PERFECT — 85 A

POTATOES
- ALMONDINE, MASHED — 90 E
- BUTTER-BAKED — 139 W
- CREAMY, WHIPPED — 81 E
- CRISPY OVEN-BAKED — 78 A
- DRESSED UP SPUDS — 79 A
- ELSIE'S — 87 E
- FLUFFY BAKED — 97 G
- GARLIC HERBED — 77 A
- HASH BROWNS — 95 E
- LATKES — 107 G
- OVEN-BAKED FRIES — 79 A
- ROASTED, HERBS — 77 A
- ROSTI — 98 G
- SKINS — 118 W
- SWEET
    - IN ORANGE — 138 W
    - SUPREME — 94 E
    - YAMMY APPLE — 146 W
- SWISS — 78 A
- SCALLOPED
    - CHEESY — 82 E
    - GRUYÈRE — 89 T
    - *LIGHTEN-UP — 88 T

"RATATOOEE" — 74 A

RICE
- BROWN & WILD — 91 T
- CASSEROLE — 105 B
- CHICKEN FRIED — 98 B
- COCONUT — 90 T
- LEMON — 80 A
- MEXICAN — 93 W
- *ORANGE — 146 T
- OVEN-BAKED — 111 G
- PILAF — 92 E
- RISOTTO — 82 A

VEGETABLES CONTINUED

RICE CONTINUED
- SAVOURY — 93 E
- WILD
    - ARTICHOKES — 154 W
    - BROCCOLI — 93 B
    - BUFFET — 110 G
    - CASSEROLE — 147 W
    - WITH MUSHROOMS — 109 G

SPINACH
- EPINARDS, EH? — 101 G
- POPEYE'S SOUFFLE — 85 E
- TIMBALES — 100 G

SQUASH
- ACORN, CHEESY — 151 W
- SPAGHETTI PRIMAVERA — 102 G
- SPAGHETTI, SPICY — 86 A

TOMATOES
- ARTICHOKE CASSEROLE — 133 W
- CHEESE BAKE — 135 W
- DILL & PARMESAN — 99 G
- FLORENTINE — 140 W
- GREEN, FRIED — 91 A
- GREEN TOMATO — 97 A
    MINCEMEAT
- *ZUCCHINI STUFFED — 85 T

TURNIPS
- 'N' APPLES — 86 E
- PUFF — 97 E

VIVA VEGGIES — 90 G

ZUCCHINI
- CASSEROLE — 99 E
- CHEESE FRIED — 152 W
- CHEESE PIE — 137 W
- ITALIAN — 112 G